Weaving Together Policies for Social Inclusion in Ireland

OECD
BETTER POLICIES FOR BETTER LIVES

LEED
BUILDING MORE & BETTER JOBS

Please cite this publication as:
OECD (2016), *Weaving Together Policies for Social Inclusion in Ireland*, OECD Publishing, Paris.
http://dx.doi.org/10.1787/9789264252677-en

ISBN 978-92-64-25266-0 (print)
ISBN 978-92-64-25267-7 (PDF)

Photo credits: Cover © iStock.com/James Brey

Corrigenda to OECD publications may be found on line at: *www.oecd.org/about/publishing/corrigenda.htm*.

Preface

Ireland has made considerable progress in rebounding from the crisis, but, like other OECD countries, it continues to grapple with how to address the lingering impacts and make growth more inclusive going forward. Addressing these challenges requires multi-faceted interventions, targeting both the most disadvantaged populations and the places where they live and work. Better understanding and addressing the relationship between people and place can lead to policies that more effectively foster social inclusion. In contrast, ignoring this relationship can lead to further entrenched disadvantage. Ireland has already undertaken a comprehensive series of reforms, and the question is now how to further build on these efforts and, as the title of this report suggests, better "weave" together the interventions already in place.

In preparing this report, the OECD's Local Economic and Employment Development Programme (LEED) looked specifically at two communities with a number of challenges that hinder social and economic inclusion. In each of these places, LEED looked across policy areas to consider three key themes: accessibility, asset-building and multi-level governance. In other words, to what degree are opportunities, programmes and services accessible to community residents? How can communities better leverage the assets that already exist, whether they be physical, human, social, financial, or cultural? And finally, how do the many interacting authority structures – spanning from the national to the local and across policy domains – interact to deliver policies, programmes and services? Policies across domains ranging from employment and skills to social innovation to the built environment are considered. Thus, mirroring the recommendations it puts forward, LEED took an integrative approach to considering the drivers of social inclusion and disadvantage.

Preparing such a report required contributions from a wide range of stakeholders, and I would like to warmly thank Pobal; the Department of Housing, Planning, Community and Local Government; the Department of Social Protection; the Department of Jobs, Enterprise and Innovation; the Department of Education and Skills; the Department of Health; the Department of Children and Youth Affairs; and SOLAS for their inputs and contributions as well as the wide range of local policymakers, practitioners, employers and residents who were engaged throughout the process.

I hope this report provides both inspiration and concrete ideas for how Ireland can further develop an integrated approach, that considers both people and places, and make growth more inclusive going forward.

Mari Kiviniemi,
Deputy Secretary-General of the Organisation for Economic Co-operation and Development

Foreword

While Ireland has made considerable progress in rebounding from the 2008 economic crash, making growth more inclusive remains a key challenge going forward (OECD, 2015a). Within the context of strong recent GDP growth and a falling unemployment rate, long-term unemployment and the rate of jobless households remain high. Ireland is not alone in grappling with these issues - countries across the OECD are increasingly recognising the importance of promoting economic growth that improves living standards and distributes the benefits of increased prosperity more evenly across social groups (OECD, 2015b).

To help understand how the fruits of economic growth can be shared more broadly, this report examines how social and economic exclusion is being addressed in Ireland, with particular attention paid to labour market exclusion. In addition to examining the national socio-economic context and policy framework, two case study areas – one urban and one rural – are examined in detail. While these case studies provide insights into the specific local context in each chosen area, more broadly, they help to paint a picture of drivers and responses to disadvantage, social exclusion and poverty at the local level across Ireland. Areas where progress has already been achieved and where further improvements could be made are both identified.

Tackling poverty and social exclusion is important not only for addressing individual-level impacts, but also because of the potential for diminished quality of life within families and across generations. The importance of parental income, education and employment for children's life chances has been well documented, and it is also evident that disadvantage and exclusion is something that can be "passed down" within families, with children whose parents have experienced long-term unemployment more likely to be unemployed, thus having knock-on effects for inclusive growth going forward.

The economic and social costs associated with failing to address social exclusion, including long- term unemployment, should not be underestimated. Individuals who are unable to reach their potential can quickly enter a poverty/welfare trap. Where disadvantage is concentrated, communities can lack cohesion and have neither the resilience to confront economic difficulties nor the ability to seize economic opportunities when they do appear. A vicious cycle of multiple disadvantages, which is difficult to break, can emerge. Whilst the costs associated with intervention can appear significant, the costs of failing to intervene, such as those associated with long-term unemployment, welfare dependency, increased offending, poor physical and mental health, and insecure accommodation, are usually even greater. In fact, recent work from the OECD suggests that a high rate of inequality actually impedes economic growth for countries as a whole (Cingano, 2014).

In examining how this cycle can be interrupted, this study focused on a number of key issues in each local case study. The findings are drawn from published statistics; interviews; facilitated roundtable discussions with a wide range of service providers and service users;

and project visits. These findings are the result of extensive collaboration between the OECD and stakeholders at the national and local level in Ireland. This includes interviews in spring 2014, a study tour in September 2014, and follow-up roundtables in June 2015.

The first issue was **accessibility**, understood as the degree to which opportunities (e.g. jobs and education), programmes and services are accessible to community residents. Physical, economic, social and psychological factors can influence access, making availability of transportation, childcare, healthcare, family services, etc. all important aspects to consider. The types of questions on which the study focused included: what opportunities, programmes, and services are available to community residents, either within or outside of the community? To what degree are these opportunities, programmes, and services accessible – in particular to people who face barriers such as unemployment, retirement, disability, family responsibilities, limited English, health issues, and/or living at a distance? How could accessibility be improved or developed?

The second issue was **asset-building**, based on the idea that all communities have strengths and resources that can be used to support sustainable development. These assets can be physical, human, social, financial, environmental, political and/or cultural. By developing the capacity of individuals, families and communities, these community assets can be better mobilised to bring about positive change. The case studies focused on the following key questions: what assets are available in the area (physical, human, social, financial, environmental, political and cultural)? Are these assets currently being leveraged? How can these assets be better developed and leveraged?

These issues align with the idea of a "capabilities approach", drawing on the work of Amartya Sen (Sen, 1999). This approach advocates that while income is important, a good quality of life and overall wellbeing requires more than this, in particular, a focus on the development and expansion of the capabilities of people. A capabilities approach emphasises functional capabilities, such as the ability to engage in economic transactions, to participate in democratic activities and to live to old age. While these capabilities can be enhanced by public policy, the direction of public policy can also be influenced by the effective use of the participatory capabilities of the public. This way of working is sometimes referred to as an "enabling state". The role of institutions is important as people's opportunities and prospects depend crucially on what institutions exist and how they function.

The final issue was **multi-level governance**. The concept of multi-level governance refers to the many interacting authority structures involved in delivering policies, programmes and services to citizens. Both vertical (the relationship between national, regional, and local level actors) and horizontal (the interaction between actors across policy areas such as employment, health, and education) aspects must be considered. The questions on which the case studies focused were as follows: to what degree do policy actors at the national, regional, and local level have the knowledge, flexibility, and resources to adequately respond to the local context? To what degree do actors across policy areas effectively co-ordinate their work? And, how could these structures be improved?

Successfully addressing social exclusion and promoting inclusive growth requires action and inputs from a wide-range of local actors, accompanied by strategies which recognise the multi-faceted nature of these challenges, particularly when inter-generational in nature. Direct interventions in the fields of education and employment can complement wider actions to build social cohesion and community capacity, whilst bottom-up, community-based initiatives have been shown to be able to successfully break the cycle of persistent unemployment and deprivation, by using communities' most valuable assets, including local talent, knowledge and resources. Harnessing the formal and informal resources that exist is central to creating effective local strategies to tackle disadvantage and promote social inclusion.

This report also draws on other recent work by the OECD which is relevant to this study. Of particular relevance and interest are reports on *Breaking Out of Policy Silos: Doing More with Less* (2010a), *Employment and Skills Strategies in Ireland* (2014a), *Local Youth Employment Strategies in Ireland* (2014b), *Improving Social Inclusion at the Local Level through the Social Economy: Designing an Enabling Framework* (2010b), *Policy Brief on Social Entrepreneurship* (2013), and the *Economic Survey of Ireland* (2015).

Acknowledgments

This review has been undertaken by the Local Economic and Employment Development Programme (LEED) of the Organisation for Economic Co-operation and Development (OECD), in co-operation with Pobal and the Department of Housing, Planning, Community and Local Government, and with the support of the European Commission Directorate General for Employment, Social Affairs and Inclusion. This publication was prepared prior to the change of the Irish Government in May 2016. However, for the purposes of clarity, the Department of the Environment, Community and Local Government is referred to by its new name, the Department of Housing, Planning, Community and Local Government, throughout this publication. Dr. Helen Johnston (National Economic and Social Council), Anna Rubin (OECD), Francesca Froy (OECD) and Antonella Noya (OECD) prepared this report. Kay Olbison was the proofreader.

The authors would also like to thank Peter Ramsden (Freiss ltd.), Andy Westwood (University of Manchester), and Max Martinez (Space Syntax) for their participation in the study tour and contributions to the report. Denis Leamy, Jerry Murphy, Catherine Morris, John Manning and Richard Deane of Pobal should also be thanked for their participation and inputs throughout the project. Additional thanks also go to Francois Iglesias, Barbara Cachova, and other colleagues in the OECD LEED Programme for their assistance with this project.

Finally, special thanks are given to the national and local representatives who participated in project interviews and roundtables, provided documentation and background materials, provided feedback on the report, and were candid and forthcoming in sharing both the strengths and challenges facing their communities.

Table of contents

Tables

Figures

Boxes

Follow OECD Publications on:

http://twitter.com/OECD_Pubs

http://www.facebook.com/OECDPublications

http://www.linkedin.com/groups/OECD-Publications-4645871

http://www.youtube.com/oecdilibrary

http://www.oecd.org/oecddirect/

Acronyms and abbreviations

AIT	Area Implementation Team
BAP	Blanchardstown Area Partnership
BTEI	Back to Education Initiative
CAMHS	Child and Adolescent Mental Health Services
CCS	Community Childcare Subvention
CE	Community Employment programme
CEDRA	Commission for the Economic Development of Rural Areas
CETS	Childcare Employment and Training Support Scheme
CLLD	European Community Led Local Development
CSO	Central Statistics Office
CYPSC	Children and Young People's Services Committees
D15	Dublin 15
DCYA	Department of Children and Youth Affairs
DDLETB	Dublin Dún Laoghaire Education and Training Board
DEIS	Delivering Equality of Opportunity in Schools
DIT	Dublin Institute of Technology
DSP	Department of Social Protection
EaSI	Employment and Social Innovation programme
ED	Electoral Division
EIF	European Integration Fund
EIT	Early Intervention Team
ERDF	European Regional Development Fund
ESF	European Social Fund
ESOL	English for Speakers of Other Languages
ETB	Education and Training Boards
EUSEF	European Social Entrepreneurship Funds
FÁS	National Training and Employment Agency
FETAC	Further Education and Training Awards Council
FIS	The Family Income Supplement
FRC	Family Resource Centre
GDA	Grangegorman Development Agency

HAP	Housing Assistance Payment
Intreo	New employment and support service
JA	Jobseeker's Allowance
JB	Jobseeker's Benefit
LCDC	Local Community Development Committee
LEC	Local Employment Co-ordinators
LECP	Local Economic and Community Plan
LEO	Local Enterprise Office
LES	Local Employment Service
NABCO	National Association of Building Co-operatives
NAPinclusion	National Action Plan for Social Inclusion 2007-2016
OFP	One-Parent Family Payment
OGP	Office of Government Procurement
PLC	Post Leaving Certificate
PPP	Personal progression plan
QNHS	Quarterly National Household Survey
RAPID	Revitalising Areas by Planning, Investment and Development programme
REDZ	Rural Economic Development Zone
RSS	Rural Social Scheme
SEETF	Social Enterprise and Entrepreneurship Task Force
SICAP	Social Inclusion and Community Activation Programme
SILC	Survey of Income and Living Conditions
SOLAS	Further Education and Training Authority
Teagasc	Irish Agriculture and Food Development Authority
Tusla	The Child and Family Agency
VEC	Vocational Education Committee
VTOS	Vocational Training Opportunities Scheme
YAP	Youth Advisory Panel

Executive summary

While Ireland has made considerable progress in rebounding from the 2008 economic crash, making growth more inclusive remains a key challenge going forward. Within the context of strong recent GDP growth and falling unemployment, long-term unemployment and the rate of jobless households remain high. To help understand how the fruits of the economic recovery can be shared more broadly and how the enduring legacies of the crisis can be resolved, this report examines how social and economic disadvantage is being addressed. In addition to examining the national socio-economic context and policy framework, two case study areas – one urban and one rural – are examined in detail. While these case studies provide insights into the specific local context in each chosen area, more broadly, they help to paint a picture of drivers and responses to disadvantage at the local level across Ireland.

National Context

While unemployment has fallen since its peak in early 2012 (9.1% in Q3 2015 compared to 15% in 2012), the latest data available (2014) shows that the rate of consistent poverty is almost twice as high as it was at its lowest in 2008 (8% compared to 4.2%). Expenditures on social welfare payments, particularly working age income and employment supports, have also grown significantly. In addition to outstanding challenges related to long-term and youth unemployment, integration of ethnic minorities and immigrants remains an issue.

As might be expected, poverty is also not distributed evenly throughout the country. The rate of consistent poverty is slightly higher in rural areas than in urban areas, although more granular analysis shows that consistent poverty and joblessness is highest in small and medium-sized towns, rather than in cities or rural areas. Regional differences in unemployment increased as a result of the economic crisis, accentuating underlying structural issues. These differentials have since narrowed, however, as the economy starts to grow again after the crisis.

A wide range of programmes are in place to deal with disadvantage at national, county and local levels. Since the economic crisis, the Irish Government has undertaken wide-ranging reforms, and there have been considerable changes in how both institutions and programmes are organised to address disadvantage. These changes are especially evident in the interface between income support for people who are unemployed, education and training options and employment support programmes (e.g. the introduction of Intreo, the establishment of Education and Training Boards). There have also been changes to mainstream service delivery which have impacted people experiencing poverty and social exclusion. In addition, there has been a major reform of local government, including the introduction of Local Community Development Committees. There are indications of the potential of social enterprises, although there is not yet a systemic vision on the role that social enterprise can play in addressing the more difficult challenges that Ireland faces.

Factors affecting the local case study areas

The Blanchardstown RAPID area has a young and growing population, characterised by high rates of ethnic diversity and a considerable migrant population. Although there are a large number of employers located in the wider Blanchardstown area, including multinational tech companies, competition for these jobs is high, and these positions tend to be filled by more highly skilled commuters. In terms of spatial layout, the swift (and planned) development of Blanchardstown has resulted in an awkward combination of a well-developed regional infrastructure of city-wide routes and services, combined with a lack of locally accessible centres and a series of housing estates which are not well linked together. At the same time, while there are many different local stakeholders working to improve the situation, this creates a rather "crowded platform" which can seem fragmented and which can dissipate resources.

North County Meath is a rural area, characterised by a relatively high age dependency ratio, a high number of one-person households, and a predominantly Irish population. Most job opportunities require commuting outside of the area, although accessibility is a problem – there are challenges in maintaining the extensive network of small roads and limited public transportation. Poor broadband connectivity and mobile phone coverage are also key challenges that have knock-on effects for issues ranging from social isolation to access to training and education, to business opportunities and economic development.

Key issues

The recent reforms in Ireland offer promise in terms of improving the ability of local actors to tackle disadvantage, and make growth more inclusive in the process. However, outstanding issues around governance and capacities remain.

More consideration is needed for how national and regional policies impact local areas in various ways (both positively and negatively). For example, land use, planning and housing allocation policies have compounded many of the issues of disadvantage which are evident in the Blanchardstown and Meath areas. In developing new social housing, more consideration needs to be given to accessibility to local services, amenities and economic opportunities, and integration into the broader urban fabric at both the local and regional scale. Many of the problems associated with Blanchardstown's growth in the past two decades can only be addressed by a coherent approach at city-regional level. This applies to decisions on inward investment, improving access to the labour market, support for immigrant integration, and social housing provision. At the same time, addressing the poor broadband infrastructure in Meath is a key priority that the county cannot tackle on its own. The roll-out of the government's new broadband strategy represents an important step forward in addressing this problem.

There is also a need to improve co-ordination between various actors working at the local level, through, for example, continuing to enhance an integrated approach to public service delivery, and the use of local brokers who act as intermediaries between organisations. In Meath, attention needs to be paid to cross-county co-ordination. As the local authorities take on their new, expanded role there is also a strong need for capacity building and more rigorous evaluation on "what works" in getting disconnected people back to work.

Both Blanchardstown and Meath have significant community assets, but they are not always leveraged to the full extent possible. The role social enterprises could play in creating job opportunities and improving service provision could be further strengthened by establishing a conducive framework at national level, while initiatives such as social innovation pilot zones could be considered. Building on ongoing efforts, private actors and employers can be better engaged in supporting local communities in meaningful ways, using tools such as social clauses in public procurement.

Early education and care requires further investment, with a priority being building a well-qualified and adequately paid early childhood workforce. Re-investing in career guidance and providing routes into employment for young people is critical.

A number of immediate priorities have been identified at the national level, and an overview of these is below. Some of these priorities already align with ongoing reform efforts. The report also identifies a number of priorities for each local case study.

Improving governance and building capacities

- **Enhance an integrated services approach.** Ireland has already taken significant steps to better integrate and co-ordinate services (e.g. establishment of Intreo and LCDCs amongst other reforms). Particular attention should be paid to how to address disadvantage at a very local level (i.e. in the "pockets" of extreme disadvantage), as more mainstream reforms on their own may not be sufficient to catalyse broader change in such communities, and may need to be complemented by locally targeted efforts.
- **Build capacities at the local level.** Local actors are now being asked to take on new responsibilities (e.g. through the LCDCs). Coupled with a diminishment in capacities at the local level as a result of the crisis (e.g. due to the freeze in public sector hiring from 2009-2014), a clear need for building local skills and capacities exists.
- **Establish a "what works centre".** Both national and local actors could benefit from having a stronger understanding of programme impacts and best practices. An independent "what works centre" (or network of centres) could play an important role in collecting and collating evaluation evidence, as well as building a stronger evidence-based policy culture.

Better leveraging of community assets

- **Support social enterprises.** Establishing a conducive ecosystem could include providing an appropriate legislative and regulatory framework; tailoring public procurement to foster the delivery of social services by promoting social clauses; facilitating access to finance; and providing capacity building opportunities to social enterprises. These efforts can complement other efforts to develop and utilise other types of community assets (voluntary associations, local schools, etc.)

Increasing accessibility to economic opportunity

- **Strengthen career guidance.** Career guidance plays an important role in helping young people develop sustainable career pathways, and the current limited provision could have longer-term implications for the labour market. In strengthening career guidance, attention should be paid to making it responsive to local and regional labour markets, as well as ensuring its provision both in and outside of schools.
- **Expand and improve apprenticeship offerings.** Work in this area is already underway through the newly established Apprenticeship Council. Going forward, it will be important for this council to consider how to expand apprenticeships to non-traditional sectors as well as how to make them accessible to disadvantaged populations, including through the provision of pre-apprenticeships and wrap-around support.
- **Improve co-ordination of migrant integration services to reduce gaps and duplication.** The co-ordination of a range of services for migrants in local communities can play a critical role in improving migrant integration. Cultural sensitivity and building authentic linkages with migrant communities will be key in making such initiatives successful. Such initiatives could bring together different services in existing facilities such as schools, and/or consist of joined up outreach carried out by different agencies in tandem. The current development of a national migrant integration strategy represents a potential avenue for addressing these issues.
- **Invest in early years education and care.** Ensuring provision is age-appropriate and of a good standard requires a well-qualified and well-paid workforce, as well as targeted support for disadvantaged children and their families.

Chapter 1

Ireland's socio-economic context

This chapter provides an overview of poverty, social exclusion and deprivation in Ireland from the mid 2000s up to the latest year data is available, 2013 and 2014 in most cases. The main groups at risk of poverty and deprivation are identified and the spatial dimension of poverty is discussed.

The 2015 OECD Economic Survey of Ireland highlights the considerable progress Ireland has made in rebounding from the economic crisis, with a robust, broad-based recovery well underway. However, more effectively tackling disadvantage and social exclusion remains a key priority if inclusive growth is to be achieved going forward. Long-term unemployment and inactivity rates have yet to recover to pre-crisis levels, and at 16.0% in 2014, Ireland had the second highest proportion of children living in jobless households out of all EU-28 countries (Eurostat, 2015).[1] Rates of consistent poverty and deprivation grew starkly between the onset of the crisis and 2013 (the most recent year data is available), and remain high in 2014. Using the most recent data available, this chapter looks more closely at the national socio-economic context, to help understand where progress has been made since the onset of the crisis and where outstanding challenges remain.[2]

Overview of poverty, social exclusion and deprivation in Ireland

Increase in poverty and deprivation

Ireland has had a national anti-poverty strategy, *Sharing in Progress,* since 1997. An agreed government definition of poverty has been in use since this time:

> *People are living in poverty if their income and resources (material, cultural and social) are so inadequate as to preclude them from having a standard of living which is regarded as acceptable by Irish society generally. As a result of inadequate income and resources people may be excluded and marginalised from participating in activities which are considered the norm for other people in society.*

This definition continues to be valid and underpins the government's strategic response to tackling poverty and social exclusion as set out in the National Action Plan for Social Inclusion 2007 – 2016 (*NAPinclusion).*

In Ireland, the government uses a **"consistent poverty"** measure, which combines living on a low income and deprivation (see Figure 1.1).[3] Poverty in the state is measured using data from the Survey of Income and Living Conditions (SILC). The latest data available (2014) shows that 8% of the population was in consistent poverty, up from 4.2% in 2008 when it was at its lowest. The Irish national social target for poverty reduction is to reduce consistent poverty to 4% by 2016 and to 2% or less by 2020.[4]

The consistent poverty measure comprises two components – at risk of poverty (income poverty) and deprivation. In 2014, 16.3% of the population was **"at risk of poverty"**, that is, living below 10 786 EUR equivalised disposable income per individual, (CSO, 2015f).[5] The percentage of people at risk of poverty has increased from 14.1% in 2009, when relative income poverty was at its lowest level, see Figure 1.2.

In terms of deprivation, nearly one third of the population (29%) experience deprivation, that is, experiencing two or more types of enforced deprivation.[6] The proportion of the population experiencing deprivation has nearly tripled in the six years to 2014, increasing from 11.8% in 2007, which was a six year low. In 2014, the types of deprivation most commonly experienced were an inability to: replace worn out furniture (25.5%), afford a morning/afternoon/evening out (22.2%) and have family/friends over for a meal/drink (19.3%).

Figure 1.1. **Conceptual measurement of poverty and deprivation**

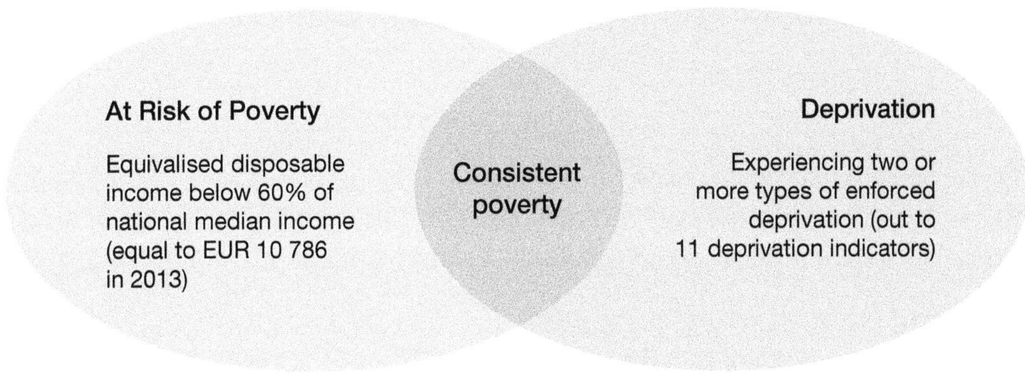

Figure 1.2. **Poverty trends (%), 2005-2014**

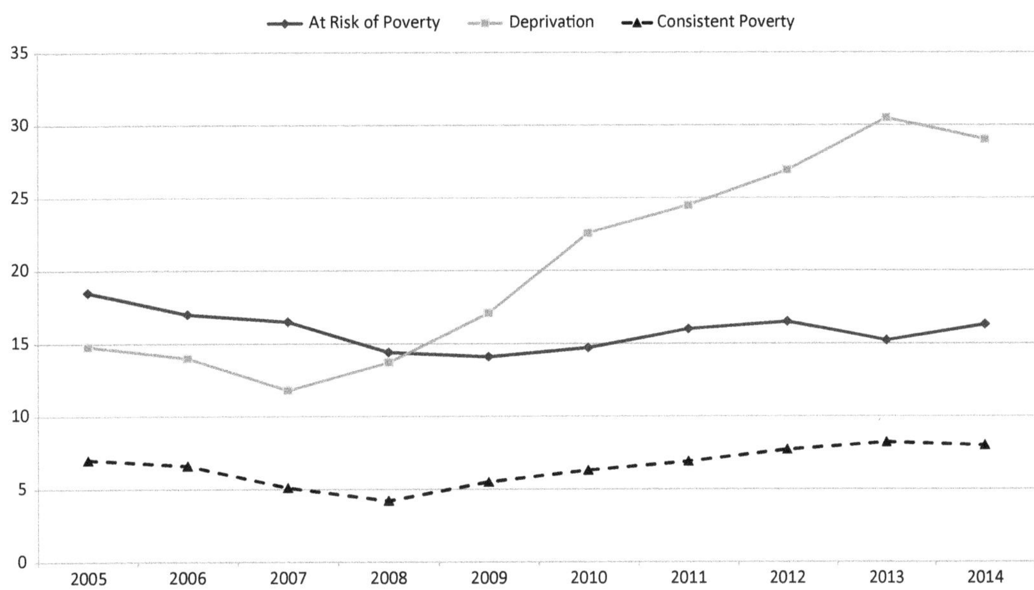

Source: CSO (2015f), SILC Results

Unemployment falling since peak in 2012

Turning to unemployment, the seasonally adjusted unemployment rate is 9.1% (CSO, QNHS, Q3 2015b), falling from a peak of 15% in early 2012. The male seasonally adjusted unemployment rate is 10.5%, while the female rate is lower at 7.4%. Long-term (more than one year) unemployment is a particular problem with the long-term unemployed accounting for 54.1% of all unemployed persons. The long-term unemployment rate was 5% (in Q3 2015), down from 9.1% in 2011. This amounts to 109 800 persons who are long-term unemployed. Youth unemployment is also an issue with one fifth (20.7%) of 15-24 year olds being unemployed (Q3 2015). In addition to those who are officially recorded as unemployed (using the ILO definition) there are substantial numbers of people who are underemployed, as well as others who are potentially attached to the labour market.[7] Figure 1.3 shows the main unemployment trends from 2006 to 2015 (Q3).

Figure 1.3. **Unemployment trends, 2006-2015**

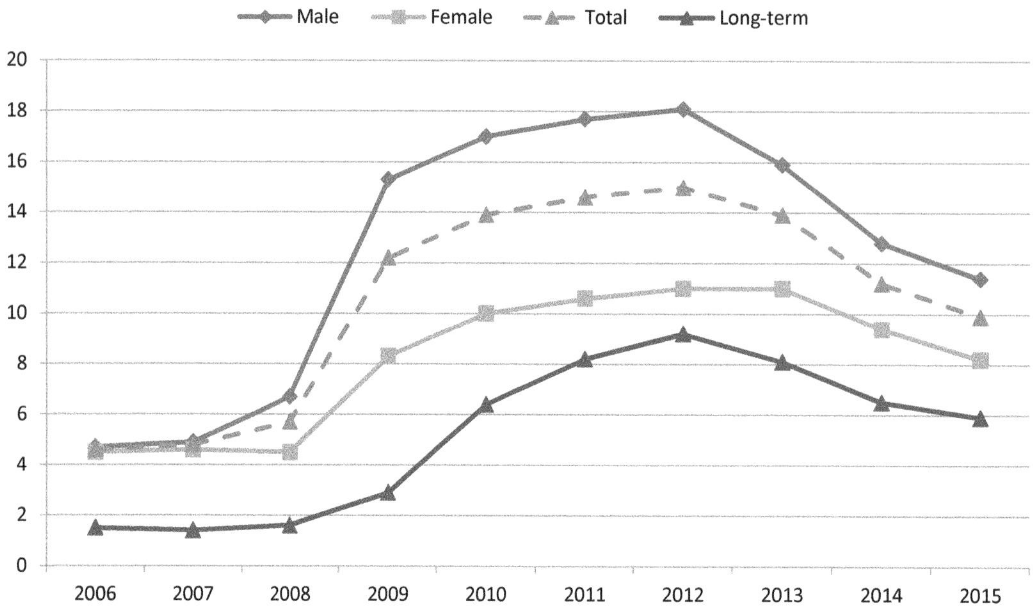

Source: CSO (2013a), Statistical Yearbook of Ireland; CSO (2015b), QNHS Q3 2015. NB. Figures for 2015 are for Q3, all other figures are annual averages.

High rate of household joblessness

Ireland has a high rate of household joblessness, where no one is working or has very limited access to work. Based on the most recent EU Labour Force Survey data, Ireland has an above average share of the adult population in jobless households – 13.5% in 2014 compared to the EU28 average of 10.9% (Eurostat, 2015). A distinguishing feature of Ireland's jobless households is the likelihood that they contain children. At 16% in 2014, Ireland had the second highest proportion of children living in jobless households out of all EU-28 countries (Eurostat, 2015).[8] As well as unemployed adults and children, jobless households contain individuals who are sick and disabled and people in caring roles, highlighting their complexity.

Waves of immigration and emigration

Ireland has traditionally been a country where many people emigrated to find work. However, with the economic boom in the early to mid-2000s, along with EU enlargement in 2004 and 2007, Ireland became a country of net in-migration, see Figure 1.4 With the onset of the economic crisis in 2008 many people left, both immigrants and young (mainly 15 to 44 year old) Irish people, so that since 2009 there has been net out-migration.

For example, in 2005 about 84 600 immigrants came to Ireland and this number grew to over 150 000 in 2007 before falling sharply to 41 800 in 2010. Since 2010 immigration has risen gradually again so that in 2014 over 60 000 people came to live in Ireland. In 2005, about 33 700 people moved to Ireland from the EU13 countries, with this number rising to 72 600 in 2007, falling back sharply to just 8 700 in 2010 and staying at about this level since.

Figure 1.4. **Migration trends, 2005-2014**

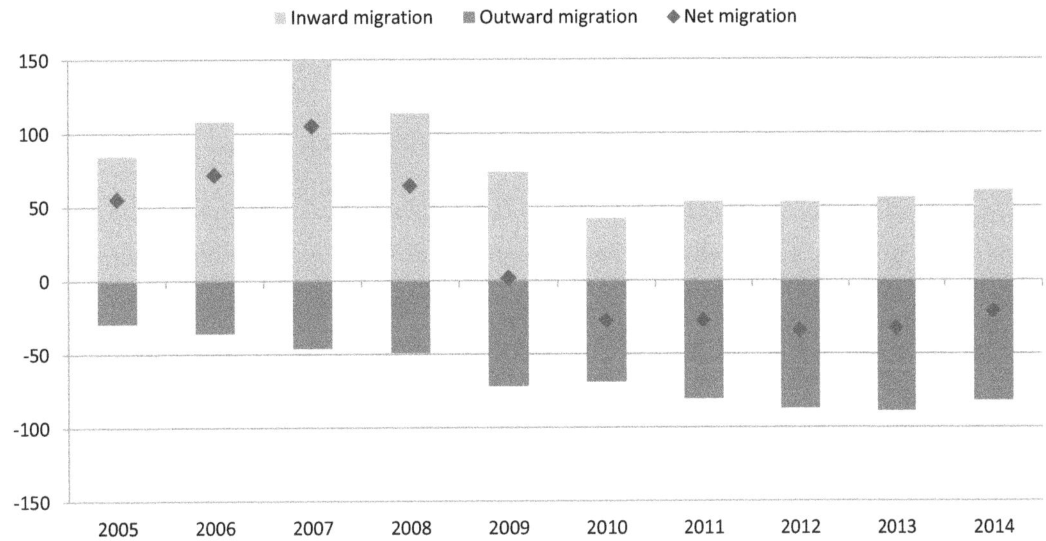

Source: CSO (2015c), *Measuring Ireland's Progress 2013*. NB. Data refer to the 12 months up to April of each year and are preliminary for 2012, 2013 and 2014. Net migration is the number of inward migrants (immigrants) less outward migrants (emigrants).

The high level of immigration during the mid-2000s has resulted in a much more ethnically diverse population in Ireland, so that in 2011 there were 544 400 non-Irish nationals of 196 different nationalities living in Ireland, with the top ten nationalities accounting for 70% of the total. Some 12% of the population in Ireland are now non-Irish nationals, with Polish nationals (122 585) and UK nationals (112 259) combined making up 5.2% of this total (CSO, 2012).

Increase in the number of recipients of social welfare payments, especially for working age income and employment supports

At the end of 2014 there were over 1.4 million recipients of a social welfare payment, paid in respect of 2.2 million beneficiaries (Department of Social Protection, 2015). The number of recipients increased by more than a third between 2007, just before the crisis, and 2014. Most of this increase was between 2007 and 2010, the height of the crisis, for most payments. Numbers in receipt of working age income supports saw a large increase between 2007 and 2010, but have been declining since. The numbers in receipt of employment supports have increased more than fivefold since 2007, but from a low base, and these continue to rise. Numbers of recipients of illness, disability and caring payments increased between 2007 and 2010, but have fallen since then. Pensions have seen a gradual increase since 2007, as the number of pensioners continues to increase. The number of children living in households dependent on social welfare payments has substantially increased since 2007, which is a worrying trend, as there is a risk of the transmission of intergenerational unemployment and poverty.[9]

Rate of poverty by population group and place

Some population groups have a high risk of being in poverty

Certain groups in the population have a particularly high risk of poverty and social exclusion, (see Figure 1.5). The rate of consistent poverty (based on low income plus deprivation) in Ireland in 2014 was 8%, being slightly higher for women at 8.3% than for men at 7.8%. Children have a higher risk of poverty than adults and older people. The reason becomes apparent when household composition is examined – lone parents have a high risk of poverty, as well as other families with children. The exception is single adults under 65 years of age who also have a high risk of poverty.

The level of educational attainment has a bearing on the risk of consistent poverty where those with low levels of educational achievement have a higher risk of poverty. In the labour market those who are unemployed have a very high risk of poverty, at 22.6%. Those who are not at work due to illness or disability, those who are on "home duties" (mainly women), and students also have a relatively high risk of poverty at more than 10%.

By and large, being in work substantially reduces the risk of poverty, although 2.4% of those aged 16 and over who are in work are at risk of consistent poverty. The impact of work is stark at the household level – with an 18.6% risk of poverty for households where no one is in work compared to a negligible risk of less than 1% where at least two people are in work. The consistent poverty risk is 8.2% where one person is in work.

These trends feed through into housing tenure with people living in housing rented below the market rate or rent free, i.e. mainly those living in local authority housing, having a much higher risk of poverty at 21.3%, than those living in other tenures. However, for those on low incomes living in private rented accommodation, rent can take up a disproportionately large amount of their income placing them at risk of poverty. Since the economic crisis, a proportion of households with large mortgage repayments may also be at risk of poverty.

Figure 1.5. **Rate of consistent poverty by population group, 2014**

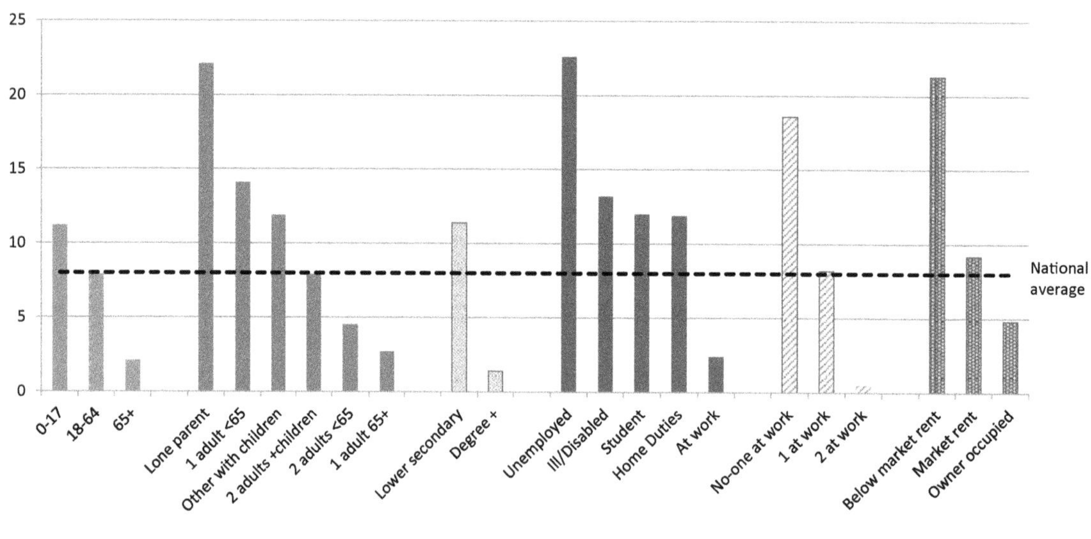

Source: CSO (2015f), SILC results

Information is not currently available on the risk of poverty for ethnic minorities. When unemployment rates are examined, however, the unemployment rate for non-Irish nationals at 11.5% was higher than the overall unemployment rate of 9.3% at this time (Q3, 2015).[10] Given the high risk of poverty associated with being unemployed it would be expected that the risk of poverty for non-Irish nationals would be higher than for the Irish national population.

As well as the risk of poverty it is useful to examine the profile of those living in consistent poverty. Figure 1.6 shows the profile of those living in consistent poverty by household composition. What is striking from this figure is the proportion of households in consistent poverty which contain children – about 75%. Figure 1.7 presents the profile of the population in consistent poverty by principal economic status. Again, the biggest proportion is children at nearly one third (31%), followed by the unemployed and those on home duties. Students and those at work each make up 11% of those in consistent poverty, while just over 6% of the consistently poor comprise those not at work because of illness or disability.

Figure 1.6. **Profile of those in consistent poverty by household composition, 2014**

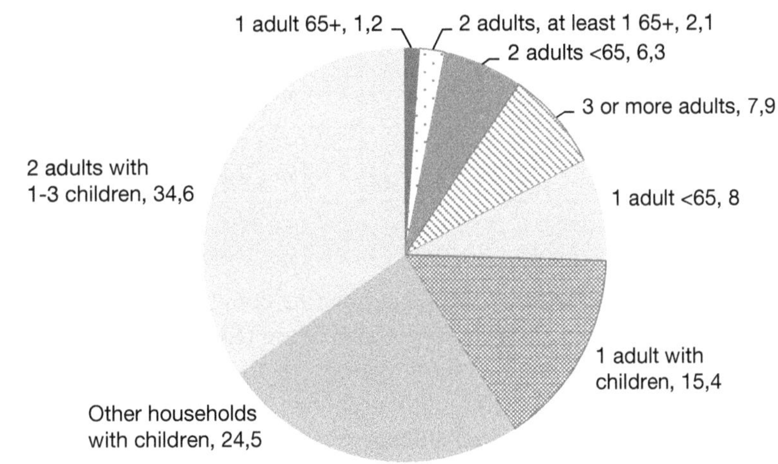

Source: CSO (2015f), SILC results

Figure 1.7. **Profile of those in consistent poverty by principal economic status, 2014**

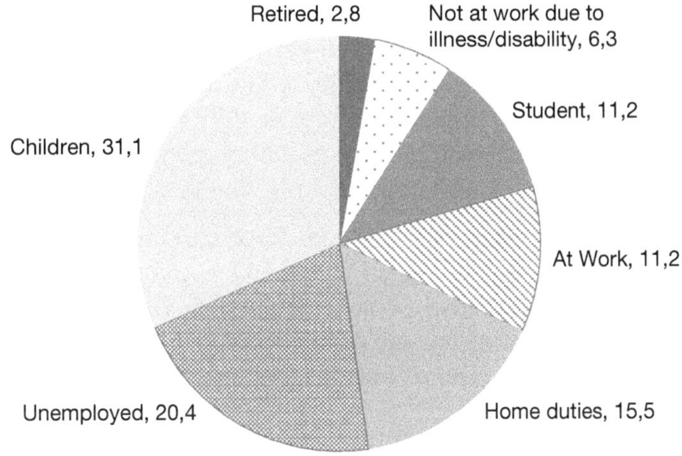

Source: CSO (2015f), SILC results

Uneven geographic distribution of poverty

As might be expected poverty is not distributed evenly throughout the country. The rate of consistent poverty (income and deprivation combined) is slightly higher in rural areas at 8.7% than in urban areas at 7.6% in 2014.[11] Further breakdown of this information shows that consistent poverty is highest in small and medium sized towns, rather than in cities or rural areas, see Table 1.1.[12] In 2011, the rate of consistent poverty in towns with a population of 1 000 to 5 000 was 10.1%, compared to 6.5% in rural areas and 4.9% in cities and their suburbs. In line with the trends observed earlier, the poverty rate was higher for children, with 14.9% of children at risk of consistent poverty in small towns (population 1 000 to 5 000).

Table 1.1. **Spatial distribution of poverty and joblessness, 2011**

	Consistent Poverty	Children in Consistent Poverty
Cities and Suburbs	4.9%	8.1%
Towns & Environs with pop. greater than 5 000	9.6%	13.2%
Towns & Environs with pop. between 1 000 and 5 000	10.1%	14.9%
Mixed Urban/Rural Areas	7.5%	8.1%
Rural	6.5%	8.3%
State	***6.9%***	***9.3%***

Source: CSO SILC (2011), Walsh, (2013) in O'Donoghue et al. (2014: Table 11).

In examining incomes throughout the state, only the counties of Dublin (EUR 22 011), Limerick (EUR 21 326), Cork (EUR 19 704) and Kildare (EUR 19 658) have a per capita disposable income which exceeds the state average of EUR 19 468 (figures for 2012). County Meath (which includes the rural study area) has a per capita disposable income of EUR 18 898, which is below the national average (CSO, 2015d).[13]

There is evidence that regional differences in unemployment increased as a result of the economic crisis. In 2007, there was a difference of two to three percentage points between the regions with the lowest unemployment rates (Midland, Mid-East and South-West regions) and the region with the highest rate (the Border region). This gap had become six to seven percentage points five years later in 2012. As the economy has begun to grow after the crisis, that differential has started to narrow again to just over four percentage points as of the third quarter of 2015 (CSO, 2007; CSO, 2015b).[14] It is noteworthy, however, that areas which had a high unemployment rate in 1991 were also likely to have a high unemployment rate in subsequent years, indicating persistent underlying structural differences (Morgenroth, 2012).

There are also regional variations in labour force participation rates.[15] For example, the participation rate in the Border region is just 56.8% compared to a national average of 60.5% (Q3, 2015). The participation rate is highest in Dublin at 63.2%. The Border region has had a tradition of working age people leaving the region in order to find work elsewhere. If this were not the case, its unemployment rate of 9.3% could be expected to be much higher.

To examine the relative degree of affluence and deprivation throughout Ireland reference can be made to the Pobal HP Deprivation Index (2011),[16] which uses indicators from the 2011 Census of Population to examine affluence and deprivation geographically (see Figure 1.8). The areas most affected by the economic recession were the outer reaches of the Dublin "commuter belt", such as Westmeath, Offaly, Laois, Louth, north Meath, Carlow and south Wicklow. Unemployment substantially increased in these areas, as did the demand for local authority housing. Other areas which were traditionally deprived, such as some local authority housing estates in Dublin, Cork and Limerick remained relatively deprived with high unemployment levels and low educational levels. The exception is the inner city docklands area of Dublin which has been regenerated and has subsequently attracted a relatively well educated and affluent population. At neighbourhood level, however, these new developments sit cheek by jowl with traditional pockets of deprivation.

Some areas of rural Ireland, such as Donegal and Mayo, show up as very deprived, with high dependency ratios as many people of working age have left to find work elsewhere. A lack of infrastructure has also been identified as an issue in these areas.

The most affluent areas remain the areas around the centres of the main cities and towns, referred to as the "traditional" commuter belt. In fact, the index has found the five main cities of Dublin, Cork, Limerick, Galway and Waterford to have been less affected overall by the recession than other areas of the country. This is reflected in their employment rate and per capita incomes, as discussed earlier.

Figure 1.8. **Affluence and deprivation in Ireland, 2006 and 2011**

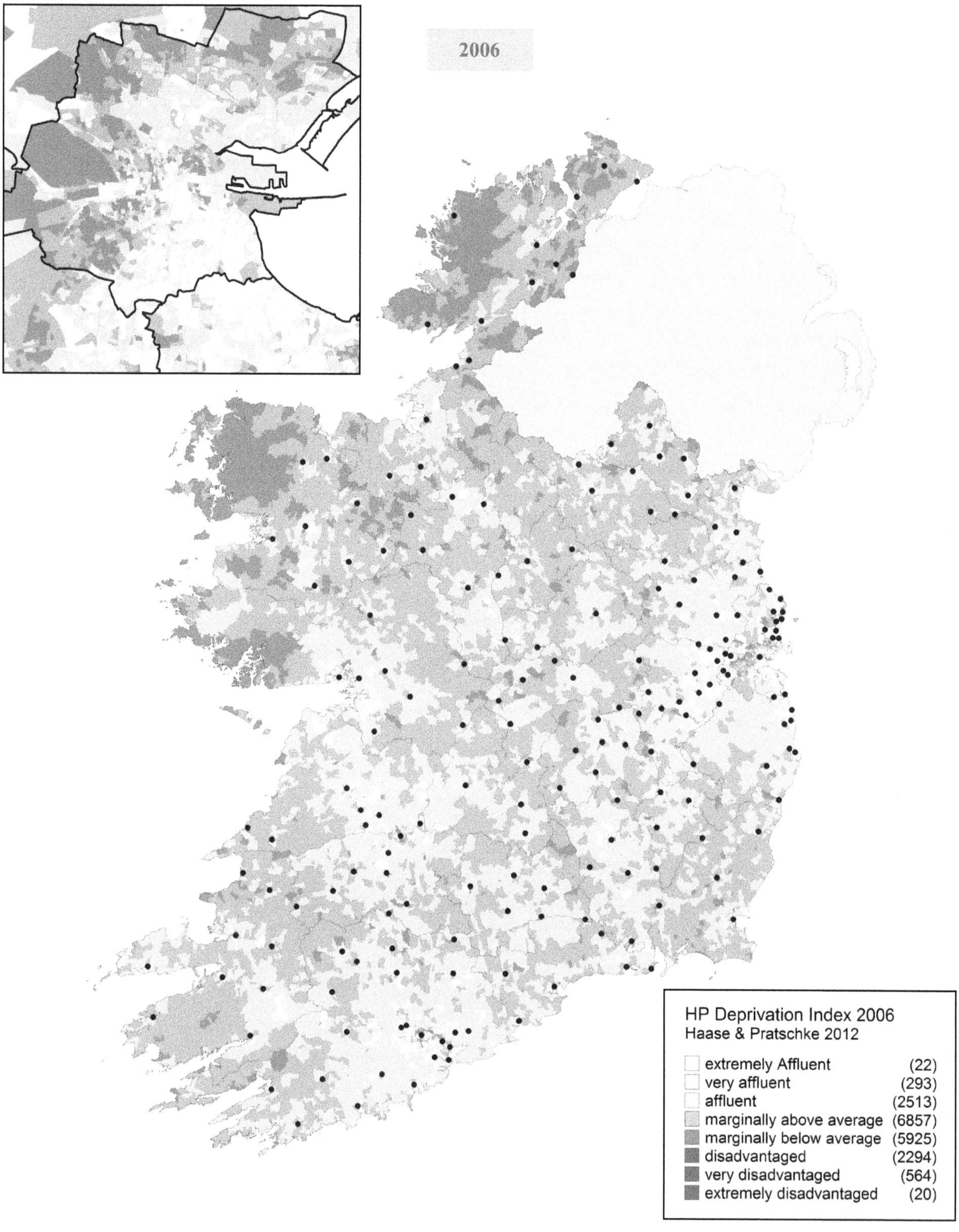

Source: Haase and Pratschke (2012), "The 2011 Pobal HP Deprivation Index for Small Areas (SA)".
Note: For the original, full colour versions, please see http://trutzhaase.eu/deprivation-index/maps/.

Figure 1.8. **Affluence and deprivation in Ireland, 2006 and 2011** *(Continued)*

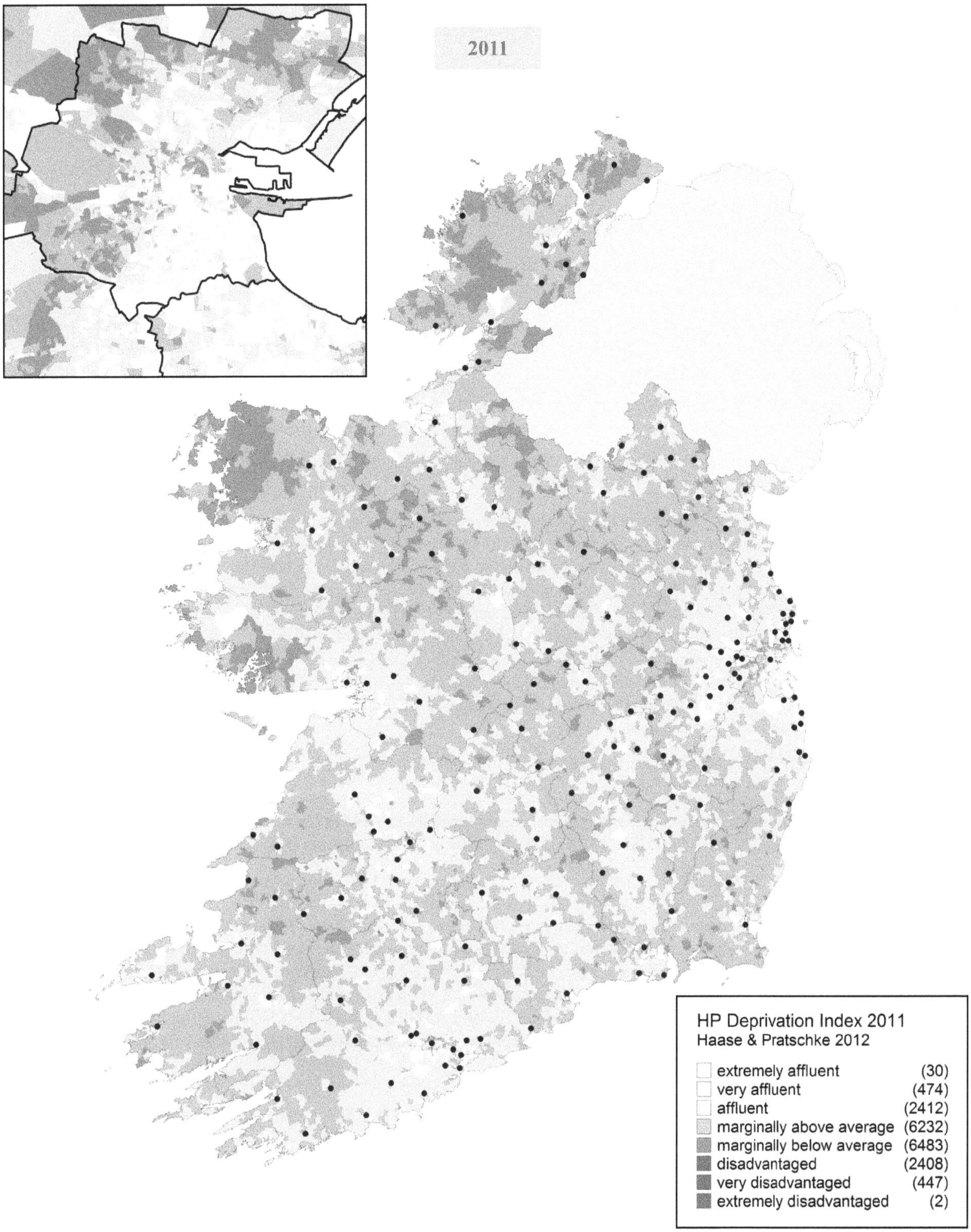

Source: Haase and Pratschke (2012), "The 2011 Pobal HP Deprivation Index for Small Areas (SA)".
Note: For the original, full colour versions, please see http://trutzhaase.eu/deprivation-index/maps/.

Notes

1. The proportion of children living in jobless households in Ireland had fallen to 14.9% by mid-2015 (CSO, 2015e). Although still high, it shows a downward trend. EU comparable data is not yet available for 2015.
2. It should be noted that where more up-to-date data is not available for the relevant indicators, these statistics do not capture the most recent impacts of Ireland's recovery on poverty, social exclusion, and inclusive growth.
3. An individual is defined as being in "consistent poverty" if they are: identified as being at risk of poverty (living below 60% of median equivalised disposable income) and living in a household deprived of two or more of the eleven basic deprivation items.
4. The national social target for poverty reduction is set at a national level. Poverty targets are not available for the case study areas. The spatial dimensions of poverty are presented in later sections of this chapter.
5. The "at risk of poverty" rate is the share of persons with an equivalised income below 60% of the national median income.
6. Households that are excluded and marginalised from consuming goods and services which are considered the norm for other people in society, due to an inability to afford them, are considered to be deprived. The identification of the deprived population is currently achieved on the basis of a set of eleven basic deprivation indicators: (1) Two pairs of warm shoes (2) A warm waterproof coat (3) Buy new (not second-hand) clothes (4) Eat meal with meat, chicken, fish (or vegetarian equivalent) every second day (5) Have a roast joint or its equivalent once a week (6) Had to go without heating during the last year through lack of money (7) Keep the home adequately warm (8) Buy presents for family and friends at least once a year (9) Replace any worn out furniture (10) Have family or friends for a drink or meal once a month (11) Have a morning, afternoon or evening out in the last fortnight for entertainment. Individuals who experience an enforced lack of two or more of the eleven listed items are considered to be experiencing deprivation.
7. For example, persons seeking work but who are not immediately available and people who are available for work but who are not actively seeking.
8. The proportion of children living in jobless households in Ireland had fallen to 14.9% by mid-2015, and the number of adults to 12.4% (CSO, 2015e). Although still high, these figures show a downward trend.
9. In 2014 there were 270 000 people on Jobseeker's Allowance, a means tested payment, 30% of whom had qualified children. Some 164 600 children live in households in receipt of Jobseeker's Allowance. There were 69 900 lone parents in receipt of One Parent Family Payment (OPFP) at the end of 2014, the majority of whom are women (98%). More than half of these households (53%) have only one child. The number of lone parents in receipt of OPFP declined by 11% between 2013 and 2014. In 2014, there were 223 300 recipients of the main disability payments. Taking the main payment (Disability Allowance with 112 100) 14% had qualified children. There were also 59400 people, mainly women (77%), in receipt of Carer's Allowance in 2014, which is a payment to people on low incomes who are looking after a person who needs support because of their age, physical/learning disability or illness.
10. Figures not seasonally adjusted.
11. The components of the consistent poverty rate show that while the "at risk of poverty rate" (using income only) is higher in rural areas than urban areas (19.1% compared to 14.6%), when deprivation is taken into account, the risk of being deprived is similar in urban (29.3%) and rural (28.6%) areas.
12. This table is based on research using the Survey of Income and Living Conditions (SILC) results for 2011, which is the most recently published information for this level of disaggregation, see O'Donoghue, C., Geoghegan, C., Heanue, K. & Meredith, D. (2014) 'The Economic Structure of Towns in Ireland', Journal of the Statistical and Social Inquiry Society of Ireland, Vol. XLIII.

13. The Blanchardstown study area is contained within the Dublin average.

14. For example, in the third quarter of 2015, the Midland region had an unemployment rate of 12.4%, while Dublin had an unemployment rate of 8%.

15. The participation rate is the number of persons in the workforce expressed as a percentage of the total population aged 15 or over.

16. The Pobal HP Deprivation Index was commissioned by Pobal from the social and economic consultants Trutz Haase and Jonathan Pratschke. The index uses a series of indicators from the Census to measure the affluence or deprivation of all parts of the country. The index includes indicators on: population change; age dependency ratio; lone parent ratio; primary education only; third level education; unemployment rate (male and female); and proportion living in local authority housing.

Chapter 2

Recent policy reforms for improving social inclusion in Ireland

This chapter presents an overview of the main policies and programmes to address poverty and social exclusion in Ireland, along with an institutional chart of the main actors involved at the national, county and local levels in delivering these policies and programmes. There have been fundamental changes in the institutional structure and the policies and programmes to tackle poverty and social exclusion since 2008, with many of these changes still in the process of being implemented.

Since the economic crisis, the Irish Government has undertaken determined reform efforts across policy areas, including those relevant to addressing poverty and social exclusion. These include reforms prompted and supported by the IMF-ECB-EU ("Troika") Programme, as well as those undertaken subsequently. Particularly significant changes have been made to the interface between income support for people who are unemployed, education and training options and employment support programmes (i.e. through the roll-out of Intreo, discussed in further detail later). There have also been changes to mainstream service delivery which have impacted people experiencing poverty and social exclusion, and major reforms of local government. While these reforms are welcome, it should also be noted that during the crisis, public resources were limited by reductions in government and public service budgets and staff numbers, along with a curtailment in many programmes which had been set up to address disadvantage.

This chapter describes the main policies and programmes for people experiencing poverty and social exclusion and the principal changes which have taken place. It also considers the national policy framework for social enterprises, including current efforts and remaining gaps. It draws on Ireland's National Social Report (Department of Social Protection, 2014), and Ireland's National Reform Programmes (Department of the Taoiseach, 2014 and 2015), as well as a recent OECD review of employment and skills strategies in Ireland (OECD, 2014a).

Institutional chart of main actors at the national, county and local levels in Ireland

There have been considerable changes in the institutions responsible for income support, employment supports, vocational education and training, child welfare, and indeed in local government since the onset of the economic crisis. A summary of the key actors most relevant for the issues raised in this report is provided in the tables below.

Table 2.1. **Selected key institutions in Ireland in the areas of income support, employment services, and enterprise services**

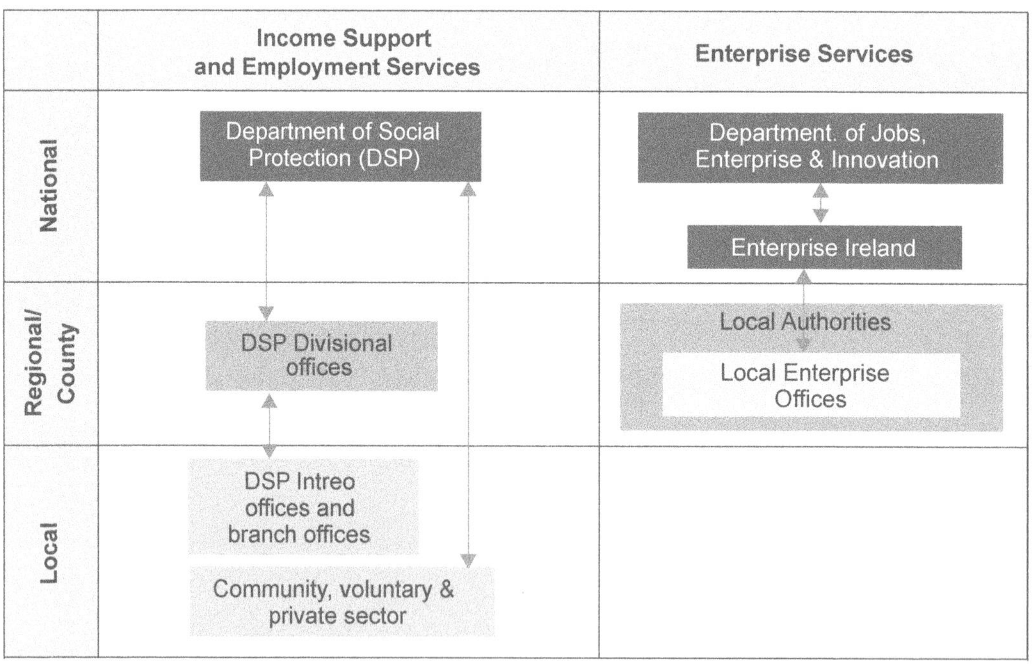

Table 2.2. **Selected key institutions in Ireland in the areas of education and training, and children and young people's services**

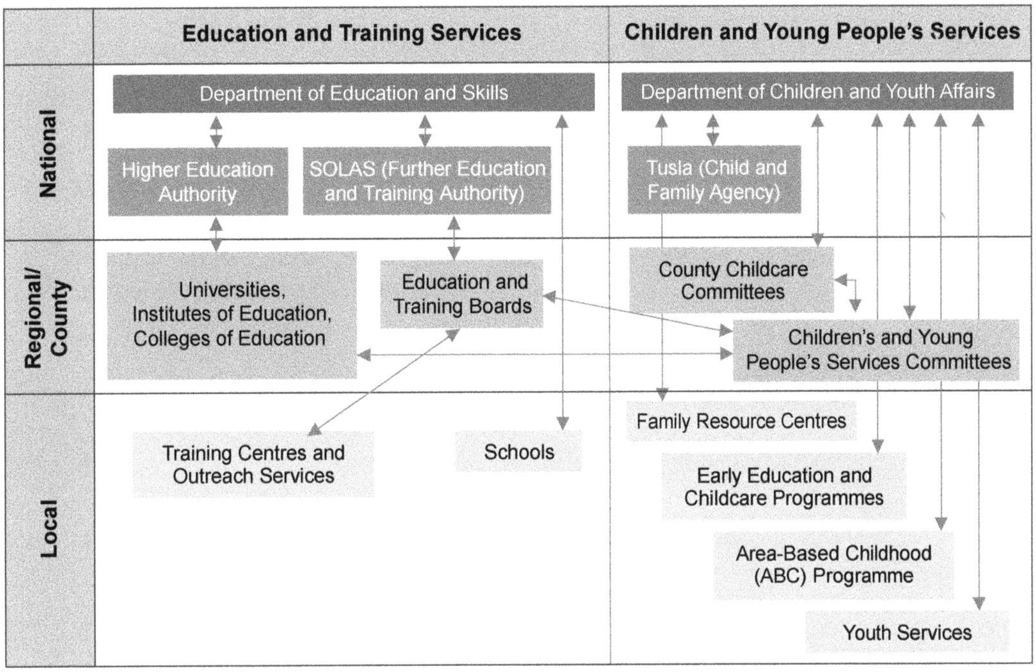

Table 2.3. **Selected key institutions in Ireland in the areas of housing, development, local development, community and rural services**

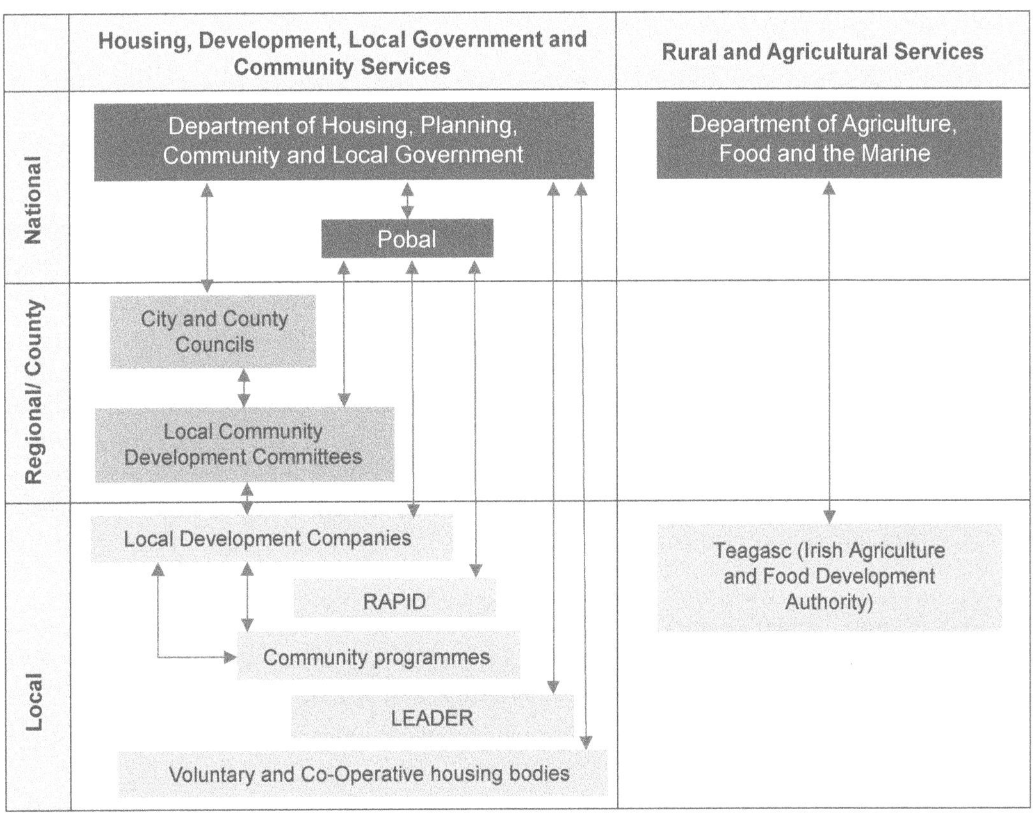

Table 2.4. **Selected key institutions in Ireland in the areas of health and justice services**

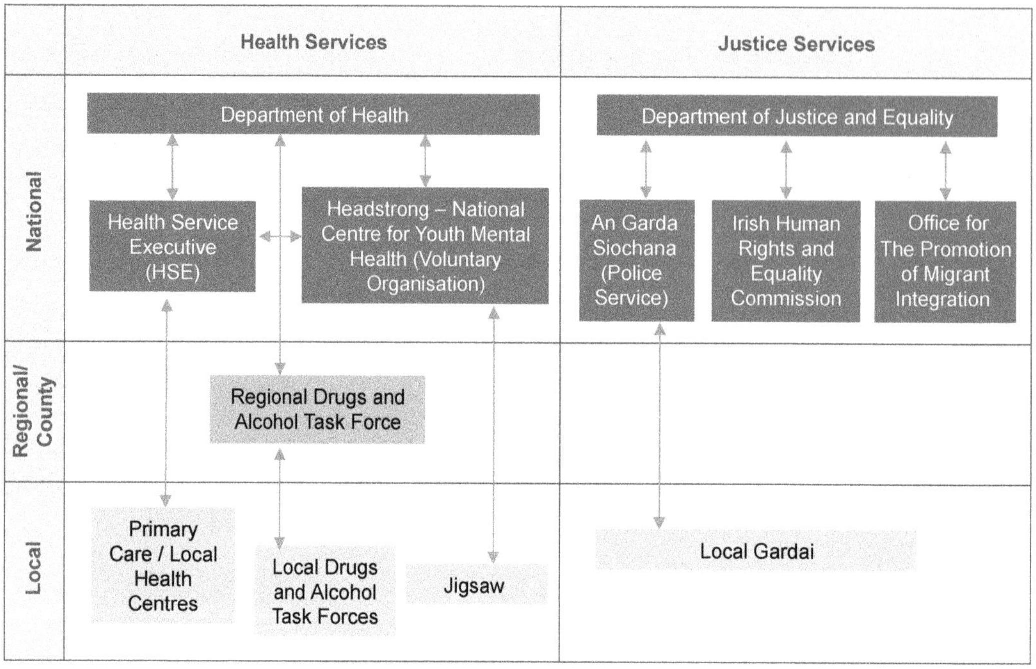

The recent changes have been summarised in the OECD publication on employment and skills strategies in Ireland (OECD, 2014a: 21). The main relevant reforms are very briefly presented here:

- **Income Support and Employment Services** – since January 2012, three services (the administration of benefits, the design and supervision of active labour market programmes, and job matching and job placement) have been rolled into one integrated service, Intreo, which is designed to adopt a stronger activation approach, see Box 2.1.
- **Local Enterprise Offices** – In April 2014 the County Enterprise Boards were dissolved under primary legislation and their functions, assets and liabilities were transferred to Enterprise Ireland. The Local Authorities, under the auspices of the Department of Housing, Planning, Community and Local Government, agreed to carry out these functions on behalf of Enterprise Ireland through the establishment of Local Enterprise Offices (LEO) in each Local Authority area. In addition to the functions legally transferred, their remit was extended to include other enterprise supports such as sign posting to other enterprise support providers and some wider local enterprise development services previously carried out within the Local Authorities themselves. The LEOs provide advice, information, training, mentoring and limited direct financial aid to micro and small enterprises.
- **SOLAS and Education and Training Boards** – the National Training and Employment Agency (FÁS) was disbanded and has been replaced by SOLAS, the Further Education and Training Authority. FÁS's network of training centres and the country's 33 Vocational Education Committees (VECs) have been amalgamated into 16 Regional Education and Training Boards.

- **Local Government Reform** – Ireland's regional and local government structures have been redrawn, with the city/county level being strengthened. The eight regional authorities and two higher tier regional assemblies have been replaced by three regional assemblies through which a slimmed down set of 31 local authorities work. Local government assumed elements of responsibility for how Ireland's large voluntary and community sector is funded. Fundamental in this reform is the role of the Local Community Development Committees, who will have a pivotal role in promoting social inclusion, see Box 2.2.[1] These new structures provide a national-regional-local-municipal route for policy formation and implementation, and should facilitate the carrying out of national policy in a focused manner in targeted areas.
- **Child and Family Services** – a Department of Children and Youth Affairs was established in 2011 to consolidate a range of functions previously discharged by a range of government departments. The Child and Family Agency (Tusla) was established in 2014, bringing together a number of agencies with a remit in the area of child welfare.

Box 2.1. **Intreo**

Intreo is the name of the Department of Social Protection service that aims to provide an integrated system of social welfare income benefits, community welfare services and employment supports. It is an amalgamation of three services which were previously provided separately. It represents one of the largest reforms of public services in recent times and involves over 7 000 staff. The Intreo service was launched in 2012, and is being rolled out on a gradual basis with the intention to have all social welfare offices providing the Intreo service.

The Intreo service represents a new approach to engaging with unemployed people, involving profiling tools and active case management. People who are unemployed and attend an Intreo service are profiled to establish their needs, such as education, training or work experience. Their probability of exit from unemployment is also assessed. These assessments determine the type of supports that will be offered, and which are set out in a personal progression plan (PPP). The PPP is an agreement between the Intreo service and the unemployed person and sets out what the employed person is expected to do and what supports the Department will provide. On this basis, a contract is signed, the "Record of Mutual Commitments", which details the unemployed person's rights with regard to the type and quality of services to be provided by the Department of Social Protection and also the unemployed person's responsibility to engage with these services and to actively seek employment. Those failing to engage in this "activation" process can have their social welfare payment reduced.

As well as providing this service through its own offices, the Department of Social Protection also provides these employment services through a number of Local Employment Services which it funds. In early 2016, private providers engaged by the Department of Social Protection will also provide these activation services for the long-term unemployed and those at risk of becoming long-term unemployed.

The Intreo service is also engaging with employers to try to ensure that unemployed people know what jobs are available and get the opportunity to apply for them. This engagement with employers is also to let employers know the range of services provided through Intreo and the skills and work experience of people who are actively seeking work.

Box 2.2. Local Community Development Committees (LCDCs)

A Local Community Development Committee has been established in each local authority area. In some local authorities there may be more than one committee. The aim of the LCDCs is to develop, co-ordinate and implement a coherent and integrated approach to local and community development.

Membership of the LCDCs is to include local councillors, local authority staff, representatives of public bodies that provide services in the area, local community representatives, and representatives of publicly funded or supported local development bodies. The majority of members must be from the non-statutory sector.

The main functions of the LCDC are to:

- Prepare the community elements of a six-year Local Economic and Community Plan;
- Co-ordinate, manage and oversee the implementation of local and community development programmes as part of implementing the Plan, e.g. the Social Inclusion and Community Activation Programme (SICAP); and
- Co-ordinate, generally, local and community development activity within the operational area of the LCDC to minimise overlap and duplication and to improve the targeting of resources.

The LCDCs were established to co-ordinate and oversee the full range of community and local development. While the initial focus, both nationally and locally, has been on the roll out of programmes such as the new Social Inclusion and Activation Programme (SICAP – see Box 2.3) and the new LEADER programme, the LCDCs are also engaged in the development of the Local Economic and Community Plans (LECPs). These plans will focus on a better targeting of resources and the promotion of a greater integration of service provision.

National social target for poverty reduction

Ireland has a National Action Plan for Social Inclusion 2007-2016 (NAPinclusion) which sets out a ten-year strategy for poverty reduction through a range of actions on income support, provision of services and innovative measures (Government of Ireland, 2007). The plan prioritises 12 high level goals in relation to children, people of working age, older people, people with disabilities and communities affected by urban and rural poverty. NAPinclusion identifies up to 150 actions across government departments and agencies with a remit in social policy, as part of a strategic approach to make a decisive impact on poverty. The achievement of some of the original high-level goals has been impacted by the economic crisis, and the plan is being updated to cover the extended period 2015-2017.

The national social target for poverty reduction is to reduce consistent poverty to 4% by 2016 (interim target) and to 2% or less by 2020, from the 2010 baseline rate of 6.3%. In recognition of the higher risks and life-long consequences of child poverty, a child-specific target has also been set. The child poverty target is to lift over 70 000 children out of consistent poverty by 2020, a reduction of at least two thirds of the 2011 level.

Within the overarching framework of the National Action Plan for Social Inclusion, the government has stated that it is committed to a co-ordinated implementation of targeted policies across all policy areas to ensure progress on the poverty target. It has adopted an "active inclusion strategy" which is based on a "developmental welfare state" approach, with the aim of placing the individual at the centre of policy development and delivery.[2] The active inclusion strategy has three main policy components:

- adequate minimum income
- inclusive labour markets
- access to quality services.

Adequate minimum income

Despite the severe fiscal crisis and substantial budget reductions, the government has sought to, by and large, maintain the rates of the main weekly social welfare payments. A report published in 2013 has shown that social transfers lifted almost 40% of the population out of poverty in 2011 (Watson and Maître, 2013). The report demonstrated that social transfers were effective in reducing poverty for all social welfare groups, ranging from 84% effectiveness for working age adults to 95% for retired people. It was 87% effective for both children and people in jobless households.

There have been payment reductions in some areas, most specifically in child income support and in jobseeker payments for young people. Nevertheless, the government has stated that it is maintaining the combined value of child income support measures at 33-35% of the minimum adult payment rate, with additions for poorer children.

There are a number of other payments targeted at supporting people on low incomes. The Family Income Supplement (FIS) is a weekly tax-free top-up payment for employees with children who are on low pay. At present, 50 300 working families with more than 111 500 children benefit from FIS (Department of Social Protection, 2015). The Advisory Group on Tax and Social Welfare has been considering the issue of working age payments with a view to smoothing the progression into employment and ensuring that "work pays".

Rent supplement is an important support for people who do not have access to a local authority provided house and cannot afford to buy or rent privately without assistance. With the onset of the economic crisis, a limited supply of local authority housing, and recent increasing rent levels especially in city areas, the demand for rent supplement has grown. The Housing Assistance Payment (HAP) scheme commenced in September 2014 and is being rolled out on a statutory phased pilot basis. Under the HAP scheme, local authorities can now provide housing assistance for households who qualify for social housing support, including many recipients of long-term rent supplement. HAP removes a barrier to employment, by allowing recipients to remain in the scheme if they gain full-time employment, it improves regulation of the rented accommodation being supported and it provides certainty for landlords as regards their rental income. Under HAP, local authorities will make the full rent payment on behalf of the HAP recipient directly to the landlord. The HAP recipient will then pay a rent contribution to the local authority. The rent contribution is a differential rent – that is, a rent based on income and the ability to pay. However, there remains the issue of supply of housing by the local authorities, along with the rising cost of many private rented properties.

Inclusive labour markets

A number of measures have been put in place to support people in getting back to work. These measures are contained in the government's *Pathways to Work* strategy, which was first launched in early 2012. In its first phase, a new integrated employment and income support service was introduced, involving the transformation of the social welfare local office network into a "one-stop shop" service called "Intreo".[3] The motivation for this major structural reform was to facilitate how jobseekers access their entitlements, while at the same time get help with planning their return to work. The main focus was on the newly-unemployed.

A second version of *Pathways to Work* began in July 2013, with a renewed focus on targeting activation places to the long-term unemployed. The second version of the strategy included the further roll-out of Intreo offices, the profiling of all new claimants, and the instigation of group and individual engagement processes, with the development of a new personal progression plan. In October 2014, *Pathways to Work* 2015 was launched. The 2015 plan commits to publicly benchmarking the performance of employment and training services against targets. There is also a particular focus on employer engagement, on long-term and youth unemployment, and the introduction of a Back to Work Family Dividend which will allow jobseekers returning to work to retain payments for their children for a set period.

There is a wide range of initiatives to support people to return to work. The main initiatives are:

- **JobsPlus** – is a recruitment subsidy which encourages employers to recruit long-term unemployed people. There are two levels of incentive: EUR 7 500 for recruits unemployed more than 12 but less than 24 months and EUR 10 000 for recruits unemployed for more than 24 months. *JobsPlus Youth* was introduced in February 2015 with a focus on the under 25s.
- **Back to Work Enterprise Allowance** – encourages people on a social welfare payment to become self-employed. People who qualify for the scheme can keep a percentage of their payment for a period of up to two years.
- **JobBridge** – is a national internship scheme that provides work experience opportunities for unemployed people. Participants in the scheme are offered an internship of six or nine months with a host organisation. If they take up an internship they will keep their social welfare payment and get an extra EUR 50 per week.
- **Gateway** – is a local authority labour activation scheme that provides short-term work and training opportunities for people who have been unemployed for more than two years.
- **Temporary Employment** – the Department of Social Protection manages a number of schemes which provide temporary employment for the long-term unemployed on works and services of value to the community. These include Community Employment and Tús.[4]
- **JobPath** – is a new labour market activation service that will be rolled out in 2016, aimed specifically at the long-term unemployed and those most at risk of becoming long-term unemployed. JobPath will be delivered by private/third party providers of employment services under contract to the Department of Social Protection.

- **Social Inclusion and Activation Programme (SICAP)** – provides educational and employment supports for the "harder to reach" in the most disadvantaged areas of the country. The programme, which is underpinned by community development approaches, is expected to support around 38 000 people and groups in 2015 and 47 000 people and groups in 2016, (see Box 2.3).

Box 2.3. Social Inclusion and Community Activation Programme (SICAP)

The Social Inclusion and Community Activation Programme (SICAP) commenced on 1 April 2015 and will run until 31 December 2017. It succeeds the Department of Housing, Planning, Community and Local Government's Local and Community Development Programme (LCDP). The aim of SICAP is to reduce poverty, promote social inclusion and equality through local, regional and national engagement and collaboration.

SICAP is a key priority of Government. The programme's target groups are: children and families from disadvantaged areas, lone parents, new communities (including refugees, asylum seekers), people living in disadvantaged communities, people with disabilities, Roma, the unemployed (including those not on the Live Register), Travellers, young unemployed people from disadvantaged areas and NEETs – young people aged 15-24 who are not in employment, education or training. There is a strong focus on community activation, social inclusion and community development, in addition to the prioritisation of those who are most hard to reach in Ireland's communities.

SICAP has three goals:

- To support and resource disadvantaged communities and marginalised target groups to engage with relevant local and national stakeholders in identifying and addressing social exclusion and equality issues;
- To support individuals and marginalised target groups experiencing educational disadvantage so they can participate fully, engage with and progress through life-long learning opportunities through the use of community development approaches; and
- To engage with marginalised target groups/individuals and residents of disadvantaged communities who are unemployed but who do not fall within mainstream employment service provision, or who are referred to SICAP, to move them closer to the labour market and improve work readiness, and support them in accessing employment and self-employment and creating social enterprise opportunities.

SICAP will receive funding of EUR 37 million in 2016 and is expected to assist 47 000 people and community groups. The funding is made up of EUR 34 million Exchequer funding and EUR 3 million European Social Fund (ESF) funding which focuses on the Youth Employment Initiative to improve employment prospects for young people aged 15-24 years, through education, skills development and employment supports.

There is also a commitment to address youth employment and social inclusion, through a Youth Guarantee. The EU-wide Youth Guarantee provides young people under the age of 25 with an offer of employment, continued education, an apprenticeship or traineeship within a short time of becoming unemployed. The Youth Guarantee is being piloted in the Dublin suburb of Ballymun, which is an area with a particularly high rate of youth unemployment. An initial evaluation of the pilot has been broadly positive, both in terms of making a contribution to a reduction in youth unemployment and in supporting the development and confidence of the young people involved (Devlin, 2015). The operation and coverage of the Youth Guarantee, in general, will be reviewed before the end of 2015, in the light of developments in the economy and in the labour market.

Reforms have been made to the One-Parent Family Payment (OFP) to encourage access to the labour market. These reforms, while recognising parental choice with regard to the care of young children, are based on the expectation that lone parents will not remain outside the workforce indefinitely. In June 2013, the Department of Social Protection introduced the Jobseeker's Allowance transitional arrangement, which caters to OFP recipients who lose their entitlement to the OFP payment, who have a youngest child aged under 14 years, and who are entitled to the Jobseeker's Allowance payment. These beneficiaries are exempt from the conditions that require them to be available for, and genuinely seeking, full-time work, but they do have to meet other conditions such as engagement with services. This exemption will remain in place until a recipient's youngest child reaches the age of 14 years. From July 2015 the age limit of the youngest child has been reduced to seven years.

Turning to education and training, the National Training and Employment Authority (FÁS) has been disbanded and replaced by a new body, the Further Education and Training Authority (SOLAS). FÁS's national network of training centres and the country's 33 Vocational Education Committees have been amalgamated in 16 regional Education and Training Boards.

Additional education and training places have been provided through a number of programmes, such as:

- The SOLAS Specific Skills Training Programme.
- The Springboard programme, which provides free, part-time higher education courses for people who are unemployed.
- The Momentum initiative, which provides education and training to assist long-term unemployed people to gain the skills they need to access work in sectors of the economy where there are job opportunities. Momentum education and training projects are free, with full and part-time projects available.
- The Back to Education Initiative (BTEI) which provides opportunities for second-chance education to adult learners and early school-leavers who want to upgrade their skills. The initiative allows learners to combine education with family, caring or work responsibilities.

There are also education and training opportunities available through Post Leaving Certificate (PLC) places, ICT graduate skills conversion courses, Youthreach,[5] the Vocational Training Opportunities Scheme (VTOS),[6] adult literacy programmes and community education. Promoting access to higher education for disadvantaged groups is also a government priority for Ireland. Several examples of coherent pathways from second-level education, from further education and other non-traditional entry routes can be found. For example, higher education institutions are pooling resources and practices to provide a regional offer for non-traditional and mature students, building on the Springboard initiative and complementing the further education offer (OECD LEED, forthcoming).

There are a limited number of apprenticeships available. A review of the Irish apprenticeship system has taken place to determine whether the current model of apprenticeships should be retained, adapted or replaced. The review of apprenticeships considered that the current system could, inter alia, be expanded into a number of other sectors and industries. An implementation plan for the recommendations of the Review of Apprenticeship Training in Ireland was published by the Minister for Education in June 2014. A new Apprenticeship Council was set up in November 2014 and made a call for proposals in January 2015 from consortia of employers and education and training providers for the development of new apprenticeships.[7] Nearly 100 proposals were received, which are being assessed by the Council. The implementation plan also seeks to accelerate the process of reviewing the curricula in existing trades.

In undertaking education, training and employment support programmes a key factor is the availability of jobs. The Government's Action Plan for Jobs (2014) focused on job creation. It paid particular attention to competitiveness, entrepreneurship, increasing exports and Foreign Direct Investment, supporting the domestic economy and improving the uptake of supports available for business. The 2015 *Action Plan for Jobs* aims at delivering full employment by 2018. Key dimensions of this plan include a focus on providing more jobs in the regions through new regional enterprise strategies, as well as new measures to help start-ups, an ambition to establish Ireland as an energy innovation hub, and efforts to reduce bureaucracy.

Access to quality services

The third policy component of the active inclusion strategy is access to quality services. Given the relatively high risk of child poverty, the emphasis in this section is placed on services for children. A Department of Children and Youth Affairs (DCYA) was established in June 2011, consolidating a range of functions focused on children which had previously been carried out by a number of government departments. The DCYA focuses on harmonising policy issues that affect children in areas such as early childhood care and education, youth justice, child welfare and protection, children and young people's participation, research on children and young people, youth work and cross-cutting initiatives for children. The DCYA has published a new strategy for children and young people, *Better Outcomes, Brighter Futures*, which is an overarching framework under which policy and services for children and young people will be developed and implemented.

In January 2014, the DCYA established the Child and Family Agency (Tusla) to support the development, welfare and protection of children, and support and encourage the effective functioning of families. It takes over the functions of a number of other agencies concerned with child welfare.

An area-based approach to tackling child poverty, referred to as the Area Based Childhood Programme (ABC), has been expanded from an initial three sites to a further ten. This programme involves interventions and services covering a broad range of areas, including parenting, early education, speech and language therapy, literacy, and pro-social behaviour.

In addition to these specific targeted programmes, the government supports the provision of early childhood and education through three childcare support programmes: the Training and Employment Childcare (TEC) programme; the Community Childcare

Subvention (CCS) programme; and the Early Childhood Care and Education (ECCE) programme. City and County Childcare Committees encourage the development of childcare services locally. A recent initiative, introduced in 2015, is "Better Start" which is an integrated national approach to developing quality in early years education and care for children aged from birth to six years. The new initiative provides a specialist on-site mentoring service. The inter-agency Children and Young People's Services Committees plan and co-ordinate services for children and young people at the county level, see Box 2.4.

Box 2.4. Children and Young People's Services Committees (CYPSCs)

Children and Young People's Services Committees (CYPSCs) are a key structure to plan and co-ordinate services for children and young people in every county in Ireland. The overall purpose is to improve outcomes for children and young people through local and national inter-agency working.

At local level, the CYPSCs are county-level committees that bring together the main statutory, community and voluntary providers of services to children and young people. They provide a forum for joint planning and co-ordination of activity and for oversight of local policy and provision, to ensure that children, young people and their families receive optimum services.

The objectives of CYPSCs are to:

- Ensure that the needs of children and young people are identified and addressed
- Plan and co-ordinate services
- Ensure effective collaboration and inter-agency working
- Promote quality, evidence-informed planning and practice
- Optimise the use of resources
- Promote best participation practice.

Further information on CYPSCs is available at www.cypsc.ie

Source: Department of Children and Youth Affairs (2015).

At school level, the Department of Education and Skills has a range of programmes in place to address educational disadvantage, collectively referred to as DEIS – Delivering Equality of Opportunity in Schools: An Action Plan for Educational Inclusion, see Box 2.5.

Box 2.5. DEIS – Delivering Equality of Opportunity in Schools

In 2005, the Department of Education brought together a number of programmes for tackling educational disadvantage under the framework of Delivering Equality of Opportunity in Schools (DEIS). DEIS remains the department's main instrument for addressing educational disadvantage, by prioritising the educational needs of children and young people from disadvantaged areas, from pre-school through second-level education (3 to 18 years).

DEIS provides a standardised system for identifying levels of disadvantage and an integrated School Support Programme (SSP). A total of 849 schools are included in the programme. These comprise 657 primary schools and 192 second level schools. In 2014 a total of EUR 141.3 million was spent on the programme - EUR 96 million by the Department of Education and Skills, EUR 24.8 million by the Department of Children and Youth Affairs, and EUR 20.3 million by the Department of Social Protection.

The School Support Programme includes a number of initiatives, such as a one-year preventative intervention scheme offered to pre-school children (3 to 4 years old) in some schools in disadvantaged areas, referred to as Early Start; the School Completion Programme, which helps students to stay in school to complete their Leaving Certificate (final school exam); a Home-School Community Liaison Scheme to improve co-operation between parents, schools and the community to address the needs of disadvantaged children; learning support teachers who provide extra support teaching for children experiencing learning difficulties, especially in the areas of literacy and numeracy; a school meals programme; and out-of-school projects for disadvantaged young people.

A recent report on learning from the evaluation of DEIS found some improvements in these disadvantaged schools in relation to planning for teaching and learning and in setting targets for achievement. There was also some improvement in literacy scores in DEIS schools, in line with improvements in literacy scores generally. There has also been some narrowing of the gap between DEIS and non-DEIS schools in some areas.

However, challenges continue to exist in relation to the adequacy of the funding to bridge the gap between disadvantaged and non-disadvantaged schools, the need for a more holistic approach to addressing educational disadvantage, and the importance of having a positive school climate.

In response to the report, the Minister for Education and Skills has committed to establishing an inter-departmental group to consider the roles of different government departments in delivering DEIS in a joined up way, as well as reviewing how disadvantaged schools are identified.

Source: Smyth, E., McCoy, S. & Kingston, G. (2015) *Learning from the Evaluation of DEIS.*

Facilitating access to housing is another key service. As alluded to earlier, the demand for housing, especially public housing in urban areas, currently exceeds supply, along with an associated affordability problem for many of those renting privately. This is resulting in increasing homelessness. There are about 90 000 households on local authority housing waiting lists and it is estimated that about 4 000 people are homeless (2014). The government published a Homelessness Policy Statement in 2013 with the stated aim to end homelessness by the end of 2016. In 2014, the government published a construction strategy, *Construction 2020*, with the objective of tackling housing shortages in Dublin, and a *Social Housing Strategy 2020*, with a commitment to provide new social housing units, as well as supporting an enhanced private rental sector and reforming social housing supports.[8] An overview of recent housing initiatives is provided in Box 2.6.

Box 2.6. **Recent housing initiatives**

In the wake of the economic crisis, the supply of housing has become a priority issue in Ireland, and a number of strategies have been published by the government in recent years.

The *Construction 2020 Strategy: A Strategy for a Renewed Construction Sector* (May 2014), sets out a cross-government plan of action which aims to put the property and construction sectors on a sustainable footing, and address any critical bottlenecks that might impede the sector in meeting the forecasted residential demand.

The *Social Housing Strategy 2020* (November 2014) sets out a comprehensive approach to the delivery of 110 000 social housing units to 2020, with a view to meeting the housing needs of the 90 000 currently on the social housing waiting lists.

A number of financial commitments have also been made, for example, Exchequer investment of EUR1.5 billion guaranteed for the period 2015 to 2017. There is also the development of a new EUR 300 million Public Private Partnership programme for social housing, and up to EUR 400 million of public investment in a new housing finance entity to leverage further substantial private investment.

In the short-term, the government is providing 500 units of modular housing for homeless families across Dublin. The programme of modular housing provision is being implemented to mitigate the issues associated with an increasing volume of homeless families being accommodated in inappropriate commercial hotel arrangements. Modular housing is being provided to offer a greater level of stability for families while move-on options to long-term independent living are identified and secured.

At a more general level, there has been an increased demand for public services, such as education and health, as a result of the economic crisis, while at the same time public expenditure on public service provision, in terms of budgets, staffing and programmes, has been reduced. These reductions have had an impact on the provision of public services.

National framework for social enterprises

Finally, social enterprises can be important actors to help the government to meet current economic and social challenges, because of their capacity to provide innovative and targeted responses to social needs, and to further sustainable economic development (Noya, 2009; OECD, 2010b). A coherent and integrated ecosystem for social enterprises, based on a systemic vision on the role of social enterprises to increase socio and economic wellbeing, still needs to be built in the country.

A number of programmes supporting social economy and social enterprise development are already being delivered, mainly through the Department of Social Protection (DSP). Among these programmes, it is worth noting the Community Services Programme introduced in 2008, to support community businesses that deliver services and create employment for people from disadvantaged groups. It provides grants to entities which are organised around the social enterprise model and which can therefore further generate their own revenues.

Other programmes, including the Community Employment Programme and the Tús and Gateway Programmes (see footnote 4 for a detailed presentation) aim at supporting the re-integration of unemployed people in the labour market by providing short-term working opportunities in the community. These programmes, run by the DSP, are implemented through community and non-profit organisations to ensure that local needs are met. Work is continuing to develop clearer progression pathways for participants of these programmes, including access to training and development.

In July 2015, the government assigned responsibility for the social enterprise agenda to Ms. Ann Phelan, T.D. Minister of State at the Department of Housing, Planning, Community and Local Government. Minister Phelan already has responsibility for rural economic development and local and community development matters, as well as implementation of the report of the Commission for Economic Development in Rural Areas (CEDRA), which identified social enterprises as assets for an integrated approach to rural economic development and provided recommendations on mobilising community capacity and supporting the potential role of social enterprises.

The recent inclusion of social enterprises in Minister Phelan's portfolio is an important step in terms of political leadership in this area and this can certainly contribute to the mission of the inter-departmental group on the social economy (referred to in the next section), which is composed of the Departments of: Housing, Planning, Community and Local Government; Social Protection; Agriculture, Food and the Marine; Health; Arts, Heritage & the Gaeltacht; and Jobs, Enterprise and Innovation.

Defining and measuring the sector

A national common definition of social enterprise does not yet exist, although Forfas[9], in its report *Social enterprise in Ireland: Sectoral opportunities and policy issues* (2013) proposed a number of criteria to help identify a social enterprise, which echo international definitions: a social enterprise should be autonomous from the government, should trade for a social purpose and earn part of its income from this trading activity, and should primarily reinvest the surplus in social objectives.[10]

In the general understanding, social enterprises are business models explicitly set up to benefit the community by tackling social, economic and environmental challenges. Most of them[11] are expected to be economically viable and therefore financially sustainable, at least in the medium and long term.

Measuring the scope and dimension of the social enterprise sector is a challenge, both at international and at national levels, for a number of reasons. These include the existence of a multiplicity of entities that claim to be, or are identified as, social enterprises within a country and, on the other hand, the variety of legal statuses and legal definitions used at international level.

The social enterprise sector in Ireland is not homogeneous and covers a number of disparate entities that tend to consider themselves, or are seen as, social enterprises, including:

- Companies limited by guarantee, the most common legal form used by social enterprises in Ireland.
- Friendly societies, which include organisations that finance welfare to specific groups.
- Credit unions, which may provide finance to social enterprises and which may themselves be considered social enterprises.
- Industrial and provident societies, the most common legal form of co-operatives.

In 2009, there were 1 420 social enterprises that employed over 25 000 people, with a total income of around EUR 1.4 billion (Forfás, 2013). Income from trading accounted for 17% of their total income. The average turnover per social enterprise was over EUR 1 million. Social enterprises are labour intensive with payroll reflecting 64% of total expenditure. The wider non-profit sector in Ireland, of which social enterprises are a subset, employs more than 100 000 people, and has an income of more than EUR 6 billion.[12] Forfás (ibid.) found that there is potential to double employment in the sector over the period to 2020.

The policy context

In Ireland, as in other OECD countries, social enterprise has entered the policy discourse in spite of an admitted "lack of understanding and awareness about social enterprises".[13] The still partial understanding of the potential role of social enterprises may stem, on the one hand, from the above mentioned difficulty of clearly identifying and measuring them, and on the other, from the different ideological approaches underpinning and motivating the development of social enterprises (Ó Broin, D, 2012).[14]

Historically, public support to the social economy started in 2000 with the Social Economy Programme. This was replaced in 2008 by the previously mentioned Community Services Programme. More recently, the development of a "vibrant social enterprises sector" was a commitment under the Government's Action Plan for Jobs in 2012. This commitment resulted in a number of actions. An important achievement was the creation of an inter-departmental group on the social economy in October 2013, following a recommendation by Forfás. The inter-departmental group is tasked with facilitating a co-ordinated governmental approach to support the development of social enterprises; with developing a policy framework for social enterprises; and with examining some of the 22 recommendations of the Forfás (2013) report, with a view to their implementation.

The establishment of the inter-departmental group could represent an important step towards the creation of a conducive ecosystem for social enterprises, especially if it is used as a policy innovation that can further foster a collaborative approach with social economy organisations (see Mendell, 2010). The inter-departmental group seems to have moved in this direction when it formally engaged with the Social Enterprise and Entrepreneurship Task Force (SEETF). The SEETF was set up in 2009 and comprises social enterprises, support organisations, community practitioners, state support organisations, academics and experts. Its main mission is to promote social enterprise and social entrepreneurship as a viable part of the Irish economy. SEETF has established, among other things, an online and social media platform, a network of social enterprises and a forum for the social enterprise community in Ireland (http://www.socent.ie/). The OECD has underlined the importance of such networks for building capacities and a sense of organisational identity (Noya, 2009).

The social economy inter-departmental group was also expected to explore mechanisms to develop capacity in the sector[15] and to advise on how best to access EU funds. The new EU Employment and Social Innovation (EaSI)[16] programme (which has a Microfinance and Social Entrepreneurship axis), and another new programme on European Social Entrepreneurship Funds (EUSEF)[17] represent important opportunities to support the development of social enterprises at the national level.[18] In order to secure financial assets for social enterprises, the inter-departmental group has also engaged with representatives from Credit Unions.

Moreover, the social economy inter-departmental group has started discussions with the Central Statistics Office on the inclusion of social enterprise in data collection, which will help to build a better understanding of the scope and the boundaries of the sector (see OECD/EC, 2013 on the importance of building such robust data sets).

The 2014 Action Plan for Jobs includes a commitment to develop the social enterprise sector based on a number of goals in the short, medium and long term, including: the policy development of the sector; building the capacity of the sector; addressing procurement policy; funding and finance; developing leaders; harnessing community support; and governance. Under the 2015 Action Plan for Jobs, and as part of the Government's Regional Action Plan for Jobs, a EUR 5 million Community Enterprise Initiatives fund has been established, which is open to groups and organisations in every county who come together with ideas for projects to create jobs.[19] Additionally, the new Social Inclusion and Community Activation Programme (SICAP), launched in April 2015, (see Box 2.3) includes support for social enterprises, and aims to strengthen the social economy and social enterprise sector, and its contribution to local development.

It should be noted that the Irish Government also provides substantial funding to social enterprises through a range of programmes and schemes, including the Community Services Programme, Community Employment Programme, the Wage Subsidy Scheme for the employment of people with disabilities, public sector contracts through the HSE and others, the Social Finance Foundation, Social Inclusion and Community Activation Programme (SICAP) and LEADER funding.

However, it is not just finance which is needed by social enterprises. Interestingly enough, according to the Department of Jobs, Enterprise and Innovation, social enterprises in Ireland do not generally seek additional state funding, but rather adjustments in policy areas such as access to finance, procurement, and conducive legislative frameworks that would help reduce barriers to their development.[20]

A reform is already underway in the area of public procurement. A social clauses project group was set up recently by the Department of Public Expenditure and Reform aimed at strengthening the use of social clauses in compliance with the EU Directive on public procurement[21] which gives member states the ability to reserve some contracts for social enterprises. This project group will put forward proposals for where social clauses could be inserted into employment and training contracts. A few experiments in the area of using public procurement as a means of creating social benefits have already been done to date, see Box 2.7.

Box 2.7. Maximising the social benefits of construction

Construction of Grangegorman Campus for Dublin Institute of Technology (DIT)

The grounds of a former mental health institution, located in Grangegorman in Dublin's north inner city, are being redeveloped as a new campus for Dublin's Institute of Technology (DIT) and for community health facilities on behalf of the Health Service Executive (HSE). This major regeneration project, on a 29 hectare (73 acre) site in a disadvantaged area, is creating in the region of 450 new construction jobs per year during the construction phase, and over 1 000 permanent new jobs upon completion.

A Grangegorman Development Agency (GDA) was established in 2006 to plan for and implement this complex, multi-phased development. The GDA, working with an Employment and Training Co-ordinator and the Labour and Learning Forum, has developed a Grangegorman Employment Charter. The purpose of the Charter is to ensure that the local community benefits from any employment opportunities that arise from the project. The Charter sets out what is required of contractors and sub-contractors in respect of employing local labour. The GDA is seeking to ensure that a minimum of 20% of new jobs created on projects will be on offer to residents of the Grangegorman neighbourhood in the first instance, and after that, of the surrounding areas. There is also an emphasis on filling 10% of new jobs created from new entrants to the labour market or the long-term unemployed.

Source: EXODEA Europe (2009), *Joining up the Dots. Study of Employment Opportunities Arising from Grangegorman Development in Dublin's North Inner City;* Grangegorman Development Agency (undated), *Grangegorman Employment Charter: Guidelines for Contractors on the Implementation and Monitoring of the Grangegorman Employment Charter,* www.ggda/employment-and-training.

Schools Construction Programme

The school-age population is increasing in Ireland and is set to continue to grow up to at least 2026 at the secondary level. This has stimulated a programme of school building projects to provide new schools and extensions to existing schools to ensure that there is sufficient school accommodation and places in the education system, now and in the future. As well as providing much needed school places, the construction of the schools and extensions is creating employment in the construction and allied sectors. As Ireland emerges from the economic crisis, when large numbers of construction jobs were lost, these building projects provide employment opportunities.

At the same time, the public procurement function is being reformed, where contractors are being encouraged to maximise the social benefits, such as employment and training opportunities, which can be delivered under social contracts. Social clauses can be used in public procurement in cases where they are targeted at issues such as employment opportunities and social inclusion. However, they must be compatible with EU law, and they must be made known to all interested parties.

One such initiative is the pilot Devolved Schools Programme. A pilot Social Employment Clause has been included in the three devolved schools bundles which are being administered by the National Development Finance Agency on behalf of the Department of Education and Skills.

Box 2.7. **Maximising the social benefits of construction** *(Continued)*

In summary, the pilot clause requires that:

- at least 10% of those working on the sites are drawn from the live register and have been unemployed for more than 12 months, and
- at least 2.5% of workers on the sites will be engaged in an approved registered apprenticeship, training or educational work placement scheme.

The general use of social clauses in public procurement is being developed by a Department of Public Expenditure/Office of Government Procurement-led working group. Findings from this pilot will assist in shaping the format of future clauses, where the pilot projects require the contractor to recruit a percentage of those employed on a public works construction site from among the long-term unemployed. While there is a long lead-time in to such projects, a small number of long-term unemployed people have been employed in these building projects.

Notes

1. Other governance reforms include the introduction of a new system of municipal districts, replacing the 80 town councils, in June 2014. The Minister for Housing, Planning, Community and Local Government made a set of orders specifying revised local electoral areas in cities and counties, and municipal districts in 25 counties giving effect to the recommendations of the independent electoral area boundary committee report published in May 2013. The municipal districts, which include towns and their hinterlands, eliminate the division caused by out-dated town boundaries and the anomaly of some small centres having a Town Council while certain other larger centres do not. The arrangements are also intended to improve operational efficiency and value for money, with a single county-wide executive and operational structure. The municipal districts are decision-making entities rather than corporate structures.

2. The "developmental welfare state" approach, promoted by the National Economic and Social Council (NESC), consists of a core structure of three overlapping areas of welfare activity: services, income supports and activist or innovative measures. Its essential character derives from the approach taken within each of these three spheres, and the integration of them in ways that are developmental for individuals, families, communities and the economy.

3. Intreo is a single point of contact for all employment and income supports and offers practical, tailored employment services and supports for jobseekers and employers, see Box 2.1.

4. The Community Employment (CE) programme is designed to help people who are long-term unemployed and other disadvantaged people get back to work by offering part-time and temporary placements in jobs based within local communities. The CE programme is administered by the Department of Social Protection, and CE sponsors (voluntary organisations and public bodies that manage CE schemes) plan and manage CE placements in local or community projects that meet a community need.
   The Tús initiative is a community work placement scheme providing short-term working opportunities for long-term unemployed people. The work opportunities are to benefit the community and are provided by community and voluntary organisations in both urban and rural areas. The Tús initiative is managed by local development companies for the Department of Social Protection, which has overall responsibility for the scheme.

5. Youthreach provides two years integrated education, training and work experience for unemployed early school leavers without any qualifications or vocational training who are between 15 and 20 years of age.

6. The VTOS scheme provides a range of courses to meet the education and training needs of unemployed people. It gives participants opportunities to improve their general level of education, gain certification, develop their skills and prepare for employment, self-employment and further education and training. VTOS is operated through the local Education and Training Boards and is aimed, in particular, at unemployed people who are early school-leavers.

7. Apprenticeship is defined by the Apprenticeship Review Group as a programme of structured education and training which formally combines and alternates learning in the work place with learning in an education or training centre, (a dual system, i.e. a blended combination of on-the-job employer-based training and off-the-job training) whose completion: a) prepares the participant for a specific occupation; and b) leads to an award, recognised under the National Framework of Qualifications from Level 5 to Level 10. The Apprenticeship Review Group stated that apprenticeships should have the following criteria:
   - Industry led
   - Two years duration as a minimum
   - Learning that alternates between a workplace and an educational or training institute
   - A minimum of 50% on the job training
   - Part of formal education and training
   - Apprentices are employed and paid under a contract of apprenticeship
   - Substantial in depth and duration, in order to prepare apprentices to work autonomously and competently in a specific occupation.

8. A number of reports on housing issues and policy have been published in recent years, including reports by NESC on *Social Housing at the Crossroads: Possibilities for Investment, Provision and Cost Rental* (2014), *Home Ownership and Rental: What Road is Ireland On?* (2014), *Ireland's Private Rental Sector: Pathways to Secure Occupancy and Affordable Supply* (2015) and *Housing Supply and Land: Driving Public Action for the Public Good* (2015).

9. Forfas is the advisory body to the government on social enterprises. It was created in 1994, but was dissolved in August 2014. Its functions have been absorbed within the Department of Jobs, Enterprise and Innovation.

10. Many definitions of social enterprise exist. The OECD in the late nineties referred to social enterprises as "...any private activity conducted in the public interest, organised with an entrepreneurial strategy but whose main purpose is not the maximisation of profit but the attainment of certain economic and social goals, and which has a capacity of bringing innovative solutions to the problems of social exclusion and unemployment" (OECD, 1999). This definition has not only influenced a number of legal definitions in some European countries but has also inspired the European Commission, which in its Social Business Initiative (SBI) aimed to create a favourable environment for social entrepreneurship. The EC defines social enterprise as: "an operator in the social economy whose main objective is to have a social impact rather than make a profit for their owners or shareholders. It operates by providing goods and services for the market in an entrepreneurial and innovative fashion and uses its profits primarily to achieve social objectives. It is managed in an open and responsible manner and, in particular, involves employees, consumers and stakeholders affected by its commercial activities".

11. It can be accepted that those social enterprises addressing particularly difficult social challenges might need to receive public financial support for long periods, and even forever, as a compensation of the particularly high social value/ social utility they deliver.

12. It is noted that these figures are for 2009, and may now be lower due to the impact of the economic crisis from 2008 to 2013.

13. Mentioned by Joan Burton, Minister for Social Protection, at the EPSCO informal council meeting during the Italian Presidency of the EU council in Milan in July 2014.

14. Joan Burton, Minister for Social Protection, stated, at the EPSCO informal council meeting during the Italian Presidency of the EU council in Milan in July 2014 that tensions exist between "a vision of needs-based or people-centred bottom-up development model and a more modest or pragmatic and top-down view of social enterprise as a labour market tool to improve the 'employability' of participants engaged at local level."

15. Capacity building for social enterprises is essential as managing a social enterprise requires not only the "traditional" skills needed to run a commercial business, but also special skills to deal with the vulnerable individuals who the social enterprise employs or serves.

16. http://ec.europa.eu/social/main.jsp?catId=1081

17. http://ec.europa.eu/finance/investment/social_investment_funds/index_en.htm

18. The EU is supporting 21 pilot projects to access social finance in different member states. More information can be found here http://social-enterprise-finance.eu/?q=about#study

19. A EUR 5 million Local Enterprise Offices (LEO) fund, covering the period 2015-2017 has also been established. The LEO Fund is open to groups of Local Enterprise Offices who come together to bid for funding for projects to support job creation in their areas.

20. www.djei.ie/press/2013/20130726.htm

21. 2014/24/EU (repealing 2004/18/EC)

Chapter 3

Blanchardstown, Ireland: Case Study on social inclusion in an urban area

This chapter examines the Blanchardstown RAPID area as a case study on social inclusion in urban areas in Ireland. Blanchardstown is a suburb north-west of Dublin with a young and growing population, characterised by high rates of ethnic diversity and a considerable migrant population. This chapter begins by providing an overview of the social and economic context for the area. Following a discussion of the current policy framework in place to improve social inclusion, it identifies a number of overarching issues that impede efforts to improve social inclusion.

Background

The urban case study is an area within Blanchardstown (a suburb north-west of Dublin), designated as a "RAPID" area. This area was designated as such by the government as part of the Revitalising Areas by Planning, Investment and Development programme (RAPID) in 2001, which targeted the most disadvantaged areas of the country where large spatial concentrations of deprivation existed.[1] The figure below shows where the case study lies within broader geographic/administrative boundaries.

Figure 3.1. **Urban case study area in context**

CASE STUDY AREA:
Blanchardstown RAPID Area
Population: 14 940
Includes parts of four Electoral Divisions: Coolmine, Corduff, Mulhuddart, and Tyrrelstown

Blanchardstown
Population: 68 000
Blanchardstown itself is the largest urban area in Fingal County Council. It has grown from a rural village on the outskirts of Dublin. During the 1970s and 1980s large local authority housing estates were built here, subsuming Blanchardstown village into a large Dublin suburb.

Dublin 15 Postal District
Population: 101 000
The postal district of Dublin 15 (D15) within Fingal County Council includes Blanchardstown as well as the Castleknock area. Over the last 10 years D15 has been one of the areas to accommodate Dublin's growing population: the population of D15 increased by 11% between 2006 and 2011 compared to an 8% increase for Ireland as a whole over this period. As a result, D15 is now a relatively young, diverse and multi-ethnic suburb of Dublin.

Fingal County Council
Population: 274 000
This local authority's administrative area covers 450 square kilometres, including both urban and rural areas and the Dublin airport. It is the second most populous county in the state, and one of the fastest growing counties in Ireland. It has the youngest population of any county and one of the highest rates of labour force participation.

Greater Dublin Area
Population: 1 801 040
The Greater Dublin Area has 39.3% of Ireland's population. The population of this area is growing rapidly and is forecast to grow to 2.1 million by 2021, and 2.4 million by 2026.

Figure 3.2. **Blanchardstown RAPID Area**

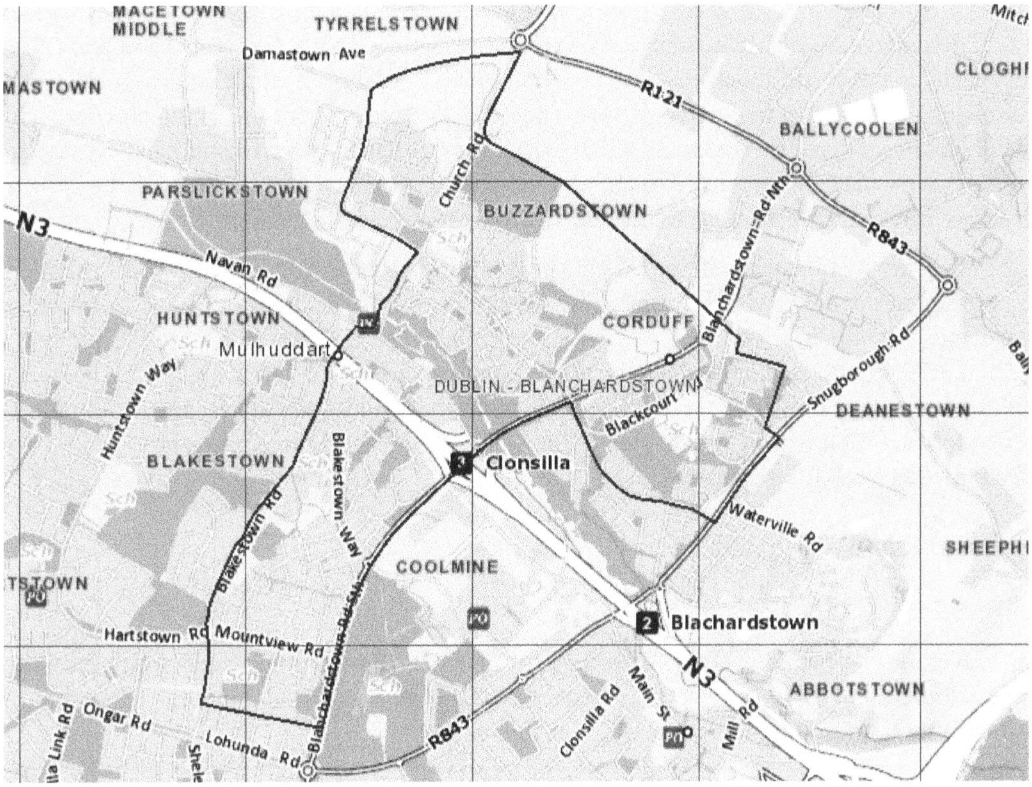

Source: Pobal, http://maps.pobal.ie/#/Map.

There are four broad areas within the Blanchardstown RAPID area: Coolmine, Corduff, Mulhuddart, and Tyrrelstown. Coolmine is to the south of the main M3 motorway which runs through the centre of Blanchardstown, while the other three lie to the north. Coolmine, also referred to as Mountview/Blakestown, comprises a number of local authority estates: Sheepmoor, Fortlawn and Whitechapel. These estates were built in the 1970s and 1980s and would traditionally have housed working class families. Many of these houses would have been purchased by the original tenants and then sold on as the original tenants who purchased them moved to other areas. Some of the houses were bought by landlords who now rent them privately. This has led to issues of maintenance and affordability.

The other three main areas within the RAPID area are north of the M3 motorway. Corduff is also a traditional local authority housing estate. As in Coolmine, many of the houses were bought by the original tenants and then sold, and are now privately rented. This estate has had a number of physical improvements recently, with new facilities being provided. Between Corduff and Mulhuddart, in Castlecurragh, there is an area of newer housing estates built during the Celtic Tiger years (early 2000s) under the "affordable housing scheme". Adult children of the people living in the surrounding local authority estates tended to buy houses here.

Mulhuddart and Tyrrelstown contain very disadvantaged estates such as Dromheath, Lady's Well, Wellview, Parnell and Avondale, and have a very diverse population. There is a mix of local authority and private rented housing, with 60% of the population of Mulhuddart renting their accommodation: over a third renting from the local authority and almost a quarter from the housing association, National Association of Building Co-operatives (NABCO).

The population of Mulhuddart and Tyrrelstown grew rapidly between 2006 and 2011, primarily in the Tyrrelstown area, and both areas have very high levels of young children and teenagers, with almost half of the population under 25. Almost one third of the population of Mulhuddart are non-Irish nationals (29%), which is more than twice the national average of 12%. For instance, the tenants of Avondale come from 24 countries of origin, with the highest number from Nigeria. There is a sizeable Traveller population in the area.

The next sections provide more background on the case study area. All information is presented for the lowest level of disaggregation possible and for the most recent data available, but much of the data was only available at the D15 level or from earlier years (e.g. 2011). Where available, data is reported at the Electoral Division level. However, because the relevant Electoral Divisions (Tyrrelstown, Corduff, Coolmine and Mulhuddart) include areas both within and outside of the designated RAPID area, statistics specifically for that area may differ slightly.[2]

Demographics

A young and growing population

Over the last 10 years, D15 has been one of the areas to accommodate Dublin's growing population: the population of D15 increased by 11% between 2006 and 2011 compared to an 8% increase for Ireland as a whole over this period.

The case study area is relatively young in comparison with Ireland more broadly. Three of Ireland's top five youngest Electoral Divisions (ED) are in D15 – Mulhuddart, Tyrellstown and The Ward – where more than a quarter of the population (26%) are aged under 15 years. By contrast, just 4.8% of the population are aged 65 and over, compared to the national average of 11.7%. As discussed above, both Mulhuddart and Tyrrelstown have very high levels of young children and teenagers.

Mainly due to the increase in young people, D15's age dependent population increased from 27.4% in 2006 to 30.9% in 2011. The Fortlawn estate in Coolmine has an overall age dependency ratio of 35.2, largely driven by a high proportion of children.

High rates of lone parents with children

Lone parents with children under 15 years of age make up 22.6% of all households in D15, and this figure is even higher in some areas. The dominant family type in Mulhuddart is two parent families with children, while in Tyrrelstown lone parent families are the dominant family type (Bookle, 2013). Some 64% of households in the Fortlawn estate in Coolmine comprise lone parents.

Considerable ethnic diversity and a large migrant population

In relation to ethnic diversity, non-Irish nationals now account for 23.5% of all residents in D15, which is almost double the state average of 12%. According to the 2011 Census, 4.3% of persons in D15 report speaking English "not well" or "not at all well". As discussed above, Mulhuddart has a particularly high rate of non-Irish nationals.

There is also an Irish Traveller population living in D15 with 658 Travellers enumerated as living here in the 2011 Census (Ryan, 2012).

Lower social class profile

An analysis of social class reveals that 40% of the population of Tyrrelstown Electoral Division (ED) is in social class 7, (unclassified) which includes those who have never been in paid employment or who live in households where the head has never been in work. Percentages in this social class are also comparatively high in the other RAPID EDs of Mulhuddart, Coolmine and Corduff at over 25%, compared to 18% for the D15 area as a whole. Between one quarter and one third of people in the RAPID area are in the skilled and semi-skilled manual social classes (4 and 5) compared to less than a quarter (23%) for the D15 area. Conversely, there are relatively few higher and lower professionals (social classes 1 and 2) in comparison with D15 as a whole (Ryan, 2012).

Greater prevalence of disability

While just under 10% of the population of D15 as a whole have a disability, 11.3% of the population of Mulhuddart have a disability, which is significant given the high levels of children and young people in the population. For example, 37% of the people with a disability in Mulhuddart were aged between 25 and 44. Higher levels of disability present greater challenges in supporting people back to work, and also requires good access to appropriate health services.

Local economy and labour market

A large number of employers, but jobs not necessarily accessible to local residents

Overall, the Dublin 15 area is well served by employers and employment opportunities. There are 27 business parks and 2 500 employers in the area. Employers include large multinational information technology and pharmaceutical companies, as well as domestic companies. For example, the Irish offices of Amazon, eBay, IBM, Nike, Puma and Wyeth are located here. There is a large shopping centre, as well as many public service employers, including a large hospital. This range of employers provides a diverse scope of employment opportunities. The area is also close to Dublin with good transport links, if travelling by car. Figure 3.3 shows the percentage of workers by industry in D15 in 2011. Commerce and trade is the largest sector at 29%, followed by professional services at 24%. It is noteworthy that only 4% were working in the building and construction industry in 2011, following the economic crash in 2008.

The jobs created in Blanchardstown over the previous two decades are within commuting distance of much of the Dublin Urban Area. As a result, there is stiff competition for jobs and local people often lose out to commuters from other areas. This is particularly true of jobs in the technology companies (e.g. Symantec, IBM, PayPal, etc.) where higher levels of education are often required, even for posts in contact centres. Efforts are being undertaken to link unemployed people in the area more closely to the jobs available (see Box 3.6 on the employer forum as one example).

Figure 3.3. **Workers by industry in Dublin 15, 2011**

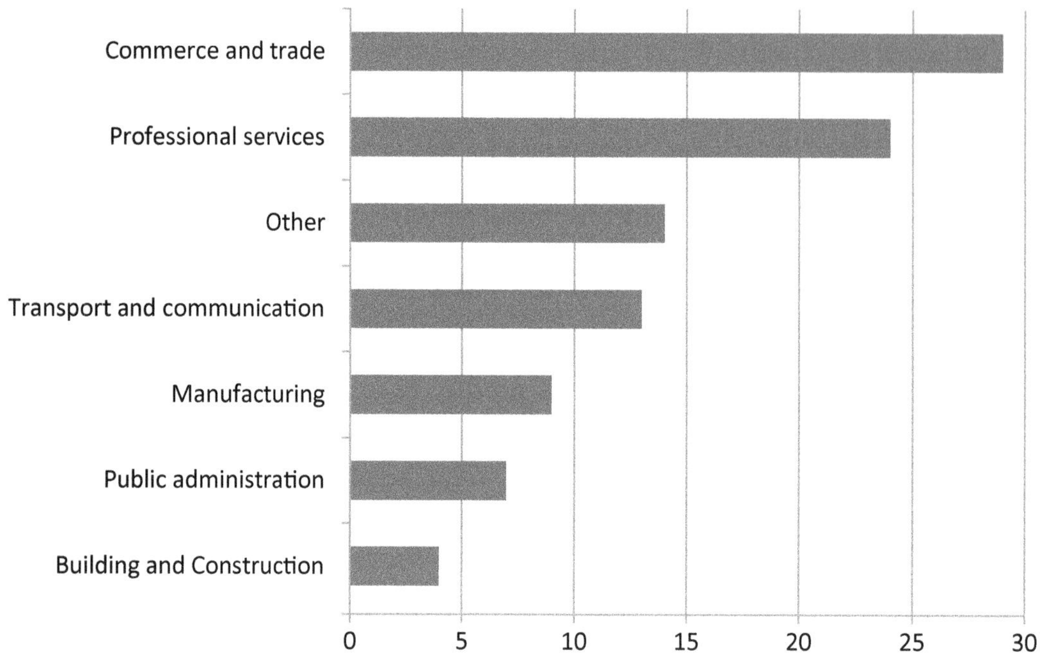

Source: Ryan (2012), "Social and Economic Profile of Dublin 15".

Pockets of particularly high unemployment rates and challenges around long-term unemployment

In 2011, the year of the most recent Census of Population, the male unemployment rate for the RAPID area was 38%, with a female unemployment rate of 28%. The most disadvantaged Fortlawn estate had a male unemployment rate of 55% and a female rate of 47%. At this level of disaggregation the 2011 Census figures are the most recent available, see Figure 3.4. The level of unemployment across Dublin 15, based on principal economic status, was 18% of the labour force in 2011 (almost doubling from 10% in 2006). This is slightly higher than the Dublin rate of 17%, but lower than the national average of 19%.

However, as the numbers of people unemployed and long-term unemployed have been falling at national level since 2012 (see Figure 1.3), some improvement could also be expected in the RAPID area. However, the extent of this improvement cannot be quantified with the data currently available.

There has been a decline in the numbers claiming unemployment benefits in the area covered by the Blanchardstown Intreo office in recent years, indicating that the upturn in the economy is reaching into the Blanchardstown estates, at least to some extent. Live Register figures for the Blanchardstown Intreo office show that there was a decline of 25% in Jobseeker's Benefit and Jobseeker's Allowance claims between July 2013 and September 2015, from 8 766 to 6 618. Approximately half of those who have left the Live Register have gone into employment, while the others have entered schemes such as the Part-time Job Incentive, Back to Work Enterprise Allowance, Back to Education, Momentum, Tús, Gateway, and JobBridge, through Intreo's activation process.[3]

Figure 3.4. **Percentage of the workforce unemployed in Dublin 15 (based on principle economic status), 2011**

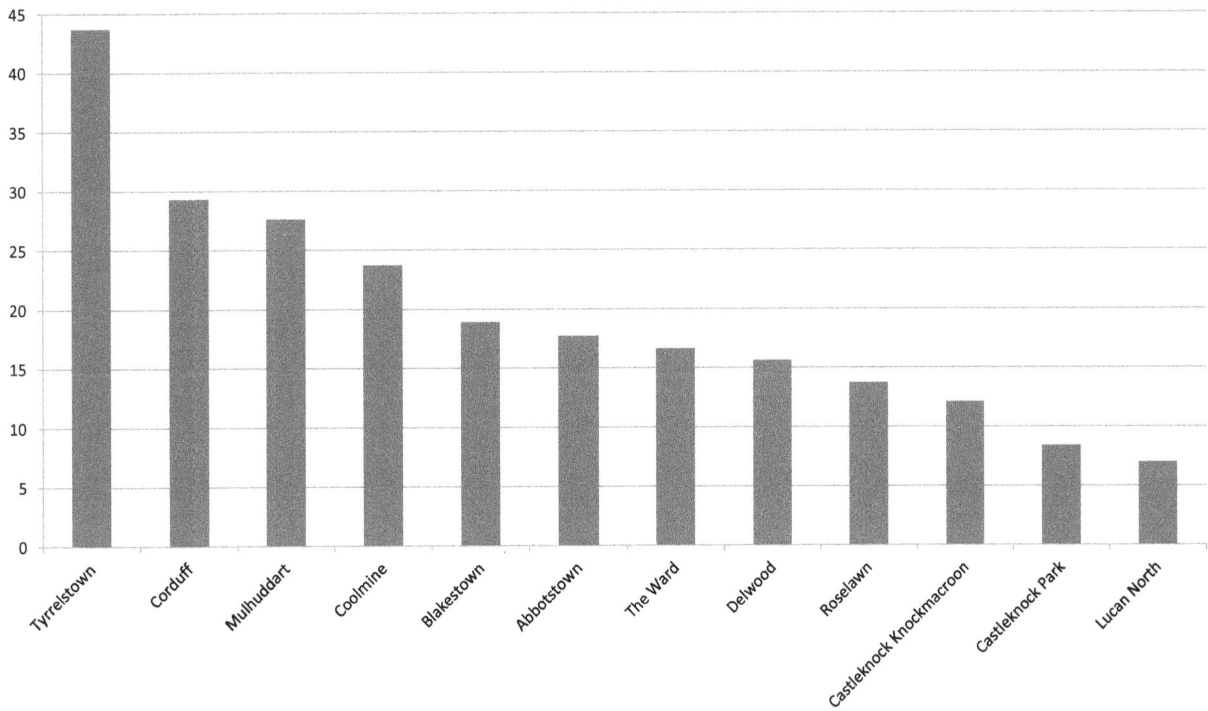

Source: Ryan (2012), "Social and Economic Profile of Dublin 15".

Although figures for D15 are not available, it is noted that unemployment levels nationally are higher among foreign nationals, at 22.4%, than among Irish persons at 18.5% (Ryan, 2012). Nearly four out of ten people (38%) on the Live Register in the Blanchardstown Intreo Office are non-Irish nationals, with 43 different nationalities signing on at this office. However, unemployment levels among foreign nationals vary significantly, where in some cases their command of the English language can determine their employability.

Labour force participation

In 2011, the total labour force of Dublin 15 was 53 394, of whom 82% were classified as "at work". Some 30 154 persons aged 15 and over were not in the labour force, with 16% retired, one fifth classified as "engaged in home duties" and just over half classed as "students". There was a marked increase in the number of students over the five year period from 2006, with more persons engaged in a post-leaving certificate course or attending a third-level faculty, reflecting the impact of the economic recession (Ryan, 2012). Between 2006 and 2011 the total number of people at work in Dublin 15 decreased by 5%. The largest percentage decline (66.7%) occurred in the building and construction sector. While more up-to-date figures are not available for employment in Dublin 15 the number of people in work at national level has grown in recent years, particularly in the construction and industry sectors, and this has been evident in the Dublin region.[4]

Low levels of educational attainment, but some signs of improvement

In the RAPID area one fifth of the population has primary education only, with only 18% having a third level qualification compared to 31% nationally. These statistics are even more stark for the Fortlawn estate with only 7% having a third level qualification and nearly one third (29%) having only a primary level of education (Census, 2011).

Social exclusion and deprivation

Concentration of deprivation in the RAPID study area

Using the HP Index of Deprivation, the relative degree of affluence and deprivation can be ascertained for the 12 EDs in D15, including those that are part of the case study area (see Table 3.1).

Table 3.1. **Areas of relative affluence and deprivation in Dublin 15, 2006-2011**

Electoral Division	2011	2006	Change in Relative Index Score 2006-2011	Relative Deprivation Score 2011
EDs in case study area				
Tyrrelstown	-13.61	-19.62	6.01	Disadvantaged
Corduff	-10.94	-10.69	-0.25	Disadvantaged
Coolmine	-3.88	-4.92	1.04	Marginally below average
Mulhuddart	-3.63	-1.91	-1.72	Marginally below average
Other D15 EDs				
Roselawn	2.61	4.09	-1.48	Marginally above average
Blakestown	2.65	3.66	-1.01	Marginally above average
Abbotstown	5.39	2.24	3.15	Marginally above average
Delwood	6.38	7.97	-1.56	Marginally above average
The Ward	7.68	9.38	1.7	Marginally above average
Castleknock-Knock-maroon	12.28	10.7	1.58	Affluent
Lucan North	14.96	16.57	-1.61	Affluent
Castleknock Park	17.27	12.16	5.11	Affluent
Dublin 15	**4.2**	**3.8**	**0.4**	**N/A**

Source: Ryan (2012), "Social and Economic Profile of Dublin 15"; Haase and Pratschke (2012), "The 2011 Pobal HP Deprivation Index for Small Areas (SA)".

Overall, the study area has a deprivation score of -11.25, with the most disadvantaged estate (Fortlawn, population 341) having a score of -20.3, compared to an average for D15 of +4.2. Within the study area, the Electoral Divisions of Tyrrelstown and Corduff suffer high levels of deprivation and are disadvantaged, while Coolmine and Mulhuddart are classified as "marginally below average". By comparison, Abbotstown, Blakestown, Delwood, Roselawn and The Ward are categorised as "marginally above average" (Ryan, 2012).

Challenges posed by drugs and crime

Another issue in this area is a drugs problem with associated intimidation and criminality. This places demands on the local health services as well as contributing to fear and distress in local communities. In addition, drugs and crime are inter-related, with an estimate that up to 85% of crime in the Blanchardstown area is drug related. While there are problems of drug use in the Blanchardstown area, much of the crime is also associated with the supply of drugs to people from outside the area, especially recreational drug users.

Adequate housing provision, but issues around affordability and maintenance

The area comprises local authority housing estates built in the 1970s and 1980s, with many of the houses now privately owned and/or rented out privately. Newer houses were built during the Celtic Tiger years of the early 2000s, through the affordable housing scheme in the Castlecurragh area. More recently the National Association of Building Co-operatives (NABCO) built houses for rent in the Avondale estate.

There are substantive numbers in receipt of a rent supplement, which is paid to people living in private rented accommodation who cannot provide for the cost of their accommodation from their own resources.[5] Figure 3.5 shows the distribution of rent supplement in Dublin with a concentration in the north and west of the city region, including Blanchardstown. In September 2013, there were 838 persons in receipt of Rent Supplement in the EDs of the RAPID area (Coolmine 453, Mulhuddart 241, Corduff 84, Tyrrelstown 60). It is notable that 1 764 persons were in receipt of Rent Supplement in Blakestown at this time. Over the past year, mainly due to rise in demand, there has been a significant increase in rents payable, creating difficulties for the administration of rent supplements subject to rent limits, especially for people dependent on social welfare benefits. A degree of flexibility has been applied locally to support families at risk of homelessness. It is notable that non-Irish nationals account for 50% of rent supplement claimants in the area.

At the time of the fieldwork for this study (2014) the provision of housing *per se* did not seem to be an issue. However, there were issues of affordability and maintenance. In some cases, young people who could no longer afford their properties were moving in with relatives, potentially leading to overcrowding, or in some cases, homelessness.

Figure 3.5. **Map of Dublin Region showing the distribution of rent supplement, September 2013**

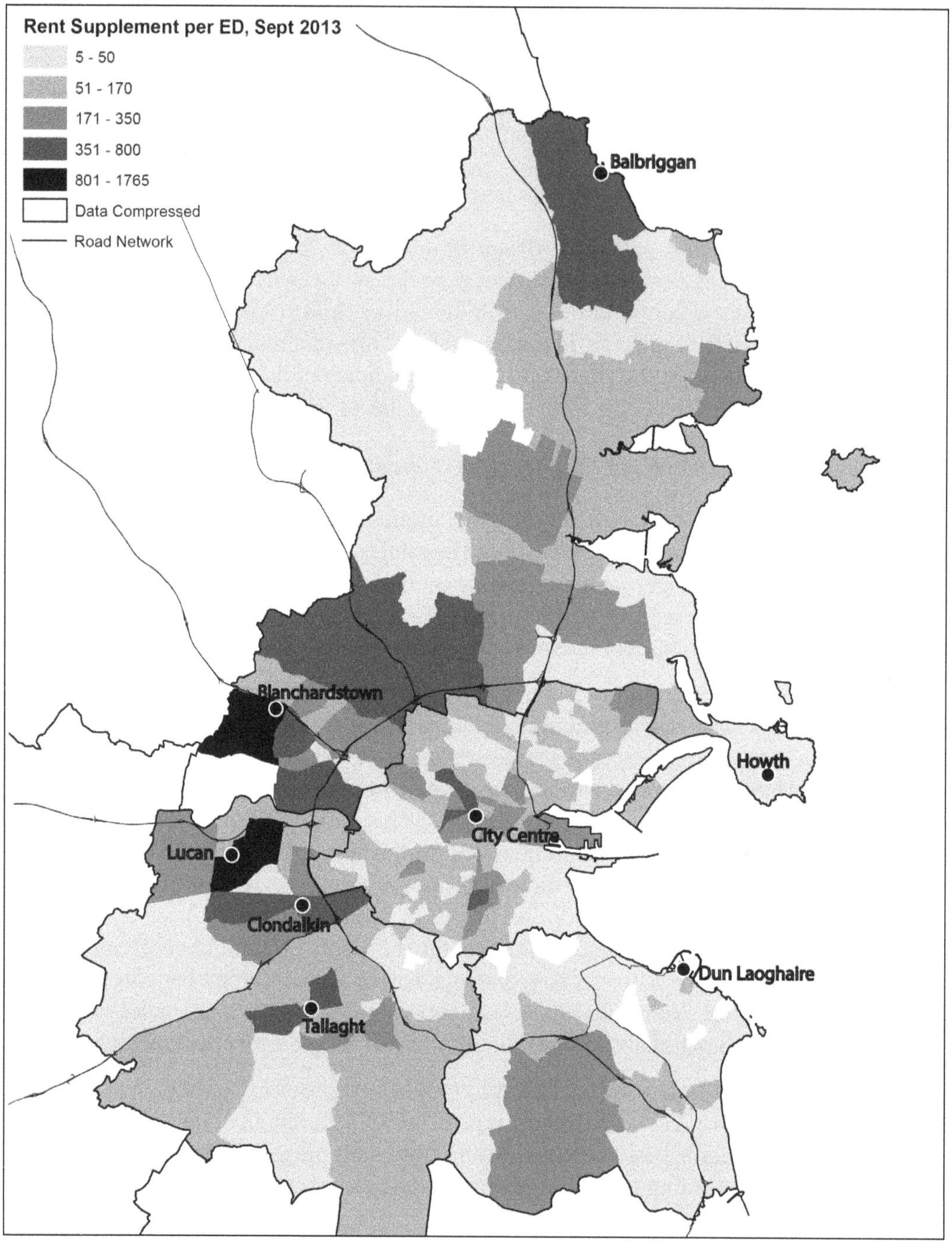

Source: AIRO, Dublin City Council Housing Monitoring Tool, http://dublindashboard.ie/pages/MappedDublinRegionHousing

Accessibility and spatial lay out

Blanchardstown has good transport links, especially for car users. There is easy access to the M50 motorway providing access links to the airport (15 minutes away) and to the motorway network to the rest of the country. The Dublin to Maynooth train stops at

Coolmine. There is a regular bus service from the city centre, though this can take some time due to traffic. However, there is limited public transport within the area and some of the routes which are there have recently been curtailed.

At the same time, there are problems associated with the spatial layout in Blanchardstown, which would seem to undermine local accessibility and also potentially impact local economic activity and community safety. As part of this project, an initial review was carried out on the potential impact of the spatial layout of each case study area in perpetuating poverty and social exclusion. An approach was used called "space syntax" (see Box 3.1).

Box 3.1. **What is space syntax?**

Space syntax is a set of techniques for representing and analysing urban street networks to uncover how these might influence human activities, most notably movement and land use. It was first developed in the late 1970s at The Bartlett, University College London and has become increasingly popular in urban planning circles as a way of ensuring that places work for people, and that the built environment does not aggravate social problems. It has been used internationally for city and regional planning, public transport strategies and spatial masterplanning of urban quarters amongst other things.

Space syntax is based on two fundamental propositions. Firstly, that space is not a background to human activity, but intrinsic to it. Secondly, that space is first and foremost configurational. In other words, what happens in individual spaces – rooms, corridors, streets and public spaces – is fundamentally influenced by the relations between that space and the network of space into which it connects.

When towns and cities emerge organically over a long period of time, a series of local centres often develop that are constituted by more accessible and well-frequented streets, where local shops and services congregate. When such local centres are also connected into more regional and global movement routes this creates a good degree of pedestrian movement and a sense of "urban buzz" – with higher numbers of both local residents and strangers (from further afield) being co-present. This can both encourage social and economic activity and also increase security through providing "natural surveillance" and reducing crime and anti-social behaviour.

In planned urban developments, the importance of connecting up local areas with each other, and simultaneously linking them into broader urban movement flows, is often missed. As a result, such places suffer from being poorly connected into the broader urban fabric, meaning that there are limited reasons for people to pass through the area, and there is a lack of pedestrian movement and natural surveillance.

Source: Hillier & Sahbaz (2009).

An infrastructure geared more to residents at the regional level, and poorly serving the local community

Blanchardstown appears to have an infrastructure that is geared more to residents at the regional level, poorly serving the local community. The rapid (and planned) development of Blanchardstown has resulted in an awkward combination of a well-developed regional infrastructure of city-wide routes and services, combined with a lack of local accessible centres and a series of housing estates which are not well linked together. Blanchardstown is now formed as a patchwork of disconnected neighbourhoods divided by a dominant traffic-oriented infrastructure, which is not easily accessible to pedestrians.

As identified in Box 3.1, healthy urban centres usually have a core of streets that have high spatial accessibility at both the city-wide and local scales. They thus mix local neighbourhood movement with large-scale movement, and this provides a good number of "passers-by", which can provide the basis for local economic and civic activities. By contrast, in Blanchardstown local and regional types of movement are kept very separate (see Figure 3.6).

Figure 3.6. **Spatial accessibility in Blanchardstown**

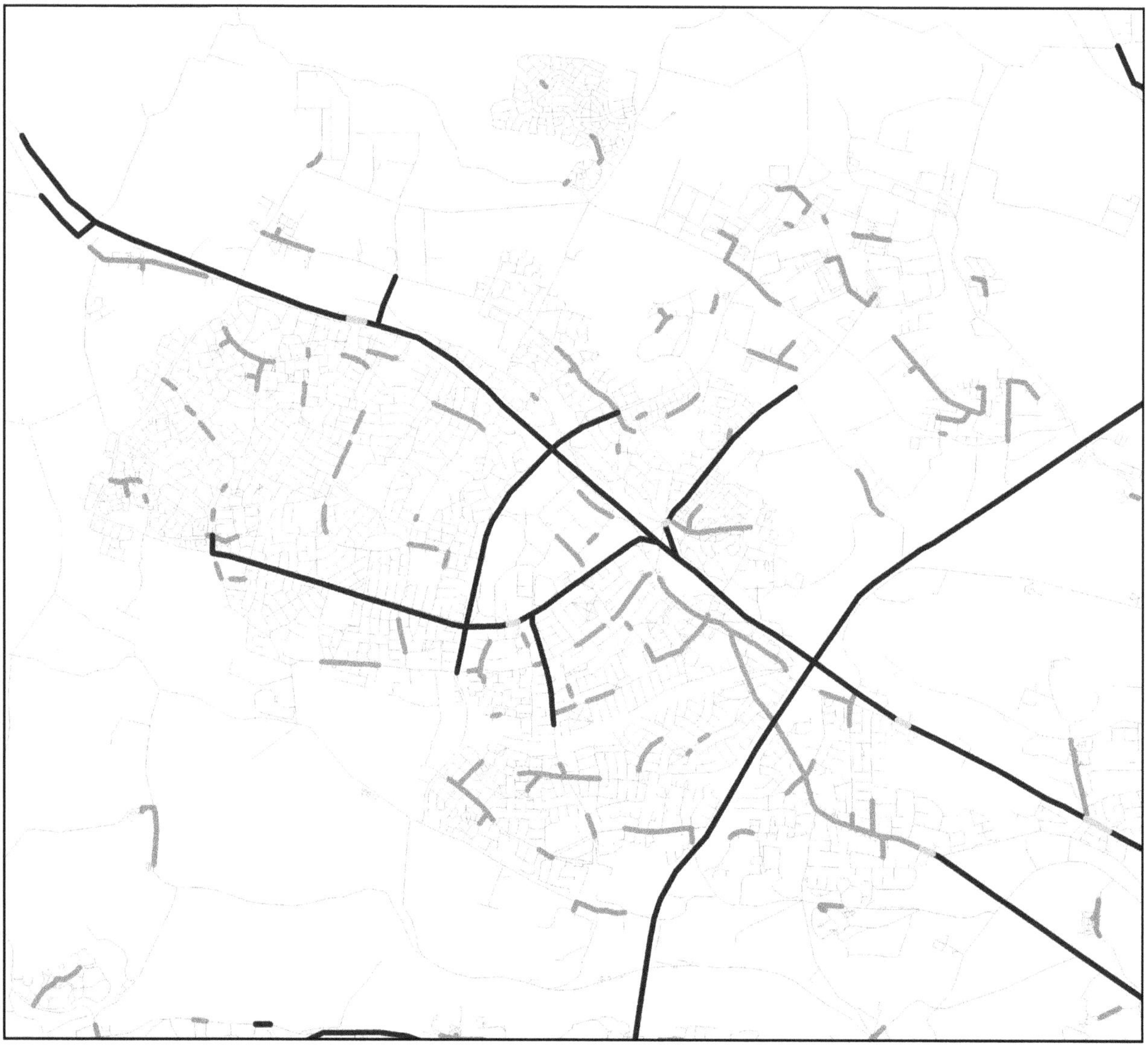

Key: Highly accessible routes at different scales:

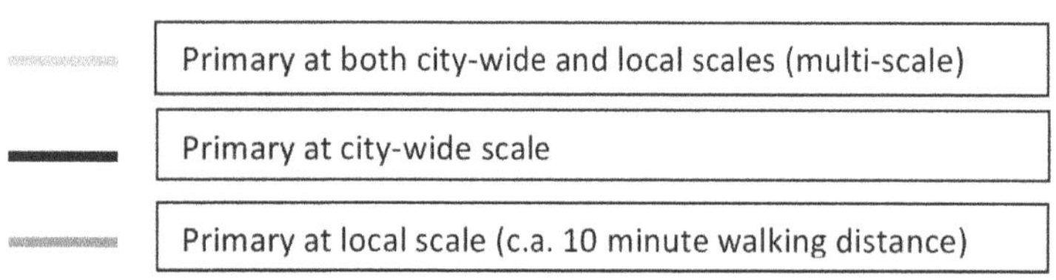

Source: Based on calculations undertaken by Space Syntax Limited

The principal roads in Blanchardstown are designed as fast urban motorways, often without any pedestrian infrastructure. Another example seen in Blanchardstown are the roundabouts that lack pedestrian crossings. The traffic-oriented infrastructure also separates, rather than joins, the different housing estates. The photo below (Figure 3.7), from Blanchardstown, shows one example of how roads are not designed for easy pedestrian movements.

Figure 3.7. **Urban road with inadequate pedestrian provision: a design focused on keeping traffic moving rather than encouraging walking**

There is also the possibility of better linking local residents to economic opportunities, both in the local area and in Dublin, through a more extensive network of cycle paths, including through simultaneous investment in bike usage (for example, bikes for hire, and subsidised bike repair support).

Lack of mixed-use areas

Commercial and infrastructure land uses are also kept separate from the local streets and estates. A number of local, national and international companies are headquartered close to Blanchardstown, however, their offices are located in industrial and business parks that are isolated from the rest of the town. Following a similar principle, Blanchardstown Shopping Centre, although located within the geographical centre of the town, has been designed as a regional shopping centre: while it is easily accessible from regional transport routes, it is an inward looking development surrounded by car parks and separated from local residential areas by large roads. This means that local residents may need a car to access the centre despite its proximity. As a private space it is also relatively exclusive, leading to an urban centre that is not accessible to all. The three train stations serving the Blanchardstown area: Castleknock, Coolmine and Clonsilla, with services to Dublin city centre, are also relatively segregated. These factors combine to reduce the number of lively public spaces locally where residents, workers, shoppers and people seeking other services can come together in the same place.

An overly permeable, segregated layout which is vulnerable to crime

Space syntax research has shown that for an urban area to be successful, the number of streets and pedestrian routes needs to correlate broadly to expected movement levels. If there is a lack of pedestrian movement around an area, and it is much dispersed, this means that the number of pedestrians in any one place will be further reduced, leading to issues such as a lack of "natural surveillance". In Blanchardstown there are currently many pedestrian footpaths and small roads in an area with relatively low housing densities meaning that the number of people walking on any one path is low. While open space can be an asset, Blanchard town also appears to have a large amount of under-used open space (sometimes referred as "slop": space left over from planning) that separates adjoining neighbourhoods and that is not sufficiently overlooked by houses. The resulting unsupervised space can become a liability and potentially increase crime levels (see Box 3.2).

An overview of community safety in the Blanchardstown RAPID area (prepared by the Local Drugs Task Force, the Dublin Institute of Technology and the RAPID co-ordinator amongst others (see McCulloch et al., 2010) found that the spatial layout of the housing estates and the design of public spaces may be exacerbating crime and anti-social behaviour. The research team found that the physical surroundings of the parks and green areas in some cases appeared to be hotspots for criminal and anti-social behaviour. Of the Community Safety Issues recorded, 144 out of a total 247 related to open spaces. Problems included people not being able to see what is ahead of them because of corners, walls, landscaping, bushes and other topographical features. The research argued the importance of increasing natural surveillance to eliminate the possibilities of blind spots, increase safety and reduce opportunities for crime.

Figure 3.8. **Left over open space between housing estates in Blanchardstown**

Box 3.2. The links between crime, anti-social behaviour and urban layouts

Space syntax research (e.g. Hillier and Sahbaz, 2009) has explored the relationship between urban layouts, crime and anti-social behaviour and shown that both crime and anti-social behaviour are inversely related to two things: the co-presence of pedestrians on the street, and the "constitutedness" of a street, i.e. whether a street is "protected" through the natural surveillance provided by numerous residential entrances and windows. In 1961, the noted urbanist Jane Jacobs highlighted the importance of natural surveillance based on her observations of daily life in New York's Greenwich Village. As people move around an area, they observe what is going on around them, provided the area is open and well lit. At the same time, residents observe these passers-by: "Eyes from the street and eyes on the street conspire to create greater safety" (Hillier & Sahbaz, 2009).

Research in three London boroughs of Tower Hamlets, Newham, and Barking and Dagenham (measuring incidents from 2005-2007) has provided further evidence of the link between urban layouts, natural surveillance and anti-social behaviour (Friedrich, Hillier, & Chiaradia, 2009). This research focused on motor-vehicle crime, property damage, drugs, dumping, violence, theft, graffiti and harassment, among other things. Anti-social behaviour was broadly spread out across "estate-type" urban layouts where there was limited pedestrian movement, a lack of continuous residential entrances opening onto streets and open spaces, and hence a lack of natural surveillance. Where there were more people present, there was more of a shared willingness to work together to intervene to prevent or stop disorder, e.g. through challenging offenders.

In summary, despite the good regional road network and transport links of the area, there are internal issues of spatial accessibility. This means that a car is required to access many of the facilities of the area, the internal bus network is limited, and many of the commercial, civic and recreational facilities are not easily accessible to the local population, especially those from the disadvantaged RAPID study area. In some areas, the design of the spaces can make criminal activity difficult to detect, resulting in an unsafe environment for local residents.

Civic amenities and community assets

The Blanchardstown area is well served by civic amenities. A civic centre comprising a theatre (Draoicht) and a library was built in 2001. There is a large shopping centre with a cinema complex and a number of retail parks. There is a large hospital, the Connolly Memorial Hospital, and a number of local health centres. The National Sports Campus is located in Blanchardstown and holds the National Aquatic Centre as well as the headquarters of Irish Sport along with facilities to accommodate a wide range of sports.

The Institute of Technology, Blanchardstown is located in the area, and the area has many primary and some secondary schools. Most of these schools are designated DEIS schools (see Box 2.5). As outlined earlier, DEIS schools receive a school support programme which includes a preventative intervention for pre-school children, home-school-community liaison, extra support for children experiencing learning difficulties, a school meals programme, a school completion programme and out-of-school projects for disadvantaged young people. In addition, a number of schools in the area have been extended, as well as new schools being built, to meet the growing school population.

However, while the area is well provided for by way of social, community, cultural and sporting facilities, in some cases their use is restricted because of limited opening hours and inadequate staffing. There is a sense that greater use could be made of some of these facilities if these shortcomings were addressed.

It is also important to acknowledge that Blanchardstown has a number of other community assets, although the degree to which they are currently being leveraged again varies. As previously described, the area is well served by employers – both multinationals and SMEs. However, local residents, particularly the most disadvantaged, are not systematically able to access the employment opportunities they provide, although the recently established Employer Forum may help in this regard.

Another major resource is the people of the area. There is much human potential and evidence of community spirit and this can be developed through personal capacity building and collective community development. There are many young people in the area, a resource which can, with support from vibrant youth and community organisations, bring energy and creativity to local areas. There is also a cohort of older people who have the potential to further develop the volunteer base to meet identified needs in the area. These needs include English language training for migrants with limited English, as well as visiting people who may be living alone or have limited mobility. The ethnic diversity of the area is also an asset, but there is an opportunity for greater engagement and interaction within and between non-Irish nationals living in the area.

The Royal Canal and Tolka Valley Park run through Blanchardstown. There is the potential to develop these assets further, both for the recreational use of local residents and to attract visitors to the area.

The current policy framework

To better understand how the issues identified above are currently being addressed, this section looks more closely at the overall local governance framework in Blanchardstown, as well as specific policy responses for social inclusion. Additionally, key gaps and challenges are identified.

General local governance framework

The Local Government Reform Act 2014 confirmed Fingal County Council as the elected body covering Blanchardstown (see Box 3.3 for a brief history of local governance changes in Blanchardstown). It has five municipal districts: Balbriggan, Castleknock, Howth–Malahide, Mulhuddart, and Swords, which is the county seat. For the purposes of elections to Fingal County Council, Blanchardstown is split between two local electoral areas. They are Castleknock (4 councillors returned) and Mulhuddart (5 councillors returned) out of a total of 40 councillors for the county. Swords is a single municipal district. Blanchardstown, along with Swords (both with populations of around 68 000 in 2011), are the largest urban areas in Ireland without their own local government and they would be the sixth largest urban area after Dublin, Cork, Limerick, Galway, and Tallaght (just larger on 71 000). Waterford is smaller at 46 000.

Prior to local government reform, the Fingal County Council was charged mainly with co-ordinating planning and housing, but will now be taking on a more central role in local and community development through the Local Community Development Committee (LCDC). It has also assumed responsibility for the RAPID area under this reform. Both are discussed in more detail in the next section.

At the regional level, Dublin is included in the Eastern and Midland Regional Assembly, established on 1 January 2015 and comprising the counties of Dublin City, Dún Laoghaire-Rathdown, South Dublin, Fingal, Louth, Meath, Westmeath, Longford, Offaly, Wicklow, Laois and Kildare. The new assemblies have powers in relation to deciding on regional spatial and economic strategies for their regions, relevant functions in relation to EU funding programmes, oversight of local authority performance, and implementing regional planning guidelines.

Box 3.3. **Brief history of local governance in Blanchardstown**

Prior to 1994, Blanchardstown was part of the administrative County of Dublin. When this administrative county was dissolved in 1994, Blanchardstown fell under the remit of the newly established Fingal County Council. Additionally, an indirectly elected Dublin Regional Authority was established that was responsible for regional planning guidance and acted as a partner in EU transnational projects, but had few other powers.

This regional authority (along with the seven other regional authorities and two regional assemblies) was dissolved in 2014 through the Local Government Reform Act. They were replaced by three regional assemblies. The Eastern and Midland Regional Assembly, established on 1 January 2015, now covers the counties of Dublin City, Dún Laoghaire-Rathdown, South Dublin, Fingal, Louth, Meath, Westmeath, Longford, Offaly, Wicklow, Laois and Kildare.

Finally, at the city-regional level the provisions of the 2014 Act would have created a directly elected mayor for a new Dublin Metropolitan Area covering the four counties of the former Dublin County. The proposal had to be agreed by the Councils of each of the four areas within the former Dublin County, (the city of Dublin and the counties of South Dublin, Fingal, and Dún Laoghaire–Rathdown) before putting the draft to a plebiscite. However, this proposal has stalled because of a "no" vote by Fingal councillors after the other three areas had voted "yes" by large majorities.

There is a variety of statutory and voluntary and community organisations working to tackle disadvantage in the area, working through local offices, community centres and local communities. Figure 3.9 provides an overview of the key actors.

Figure 3.9. **Selected key institutional actors in the Blanchardstown RAPID Area**

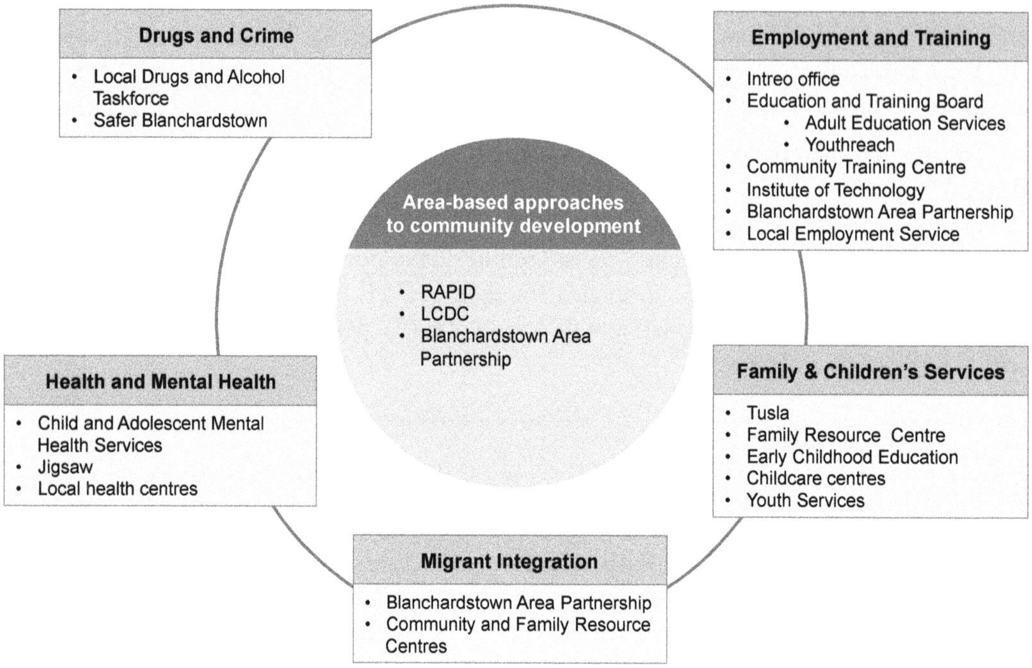

Area based approaches to community development

Within Blanchardstown, there are a number of organisations taking an area-based approach to community development. The LCDC has been set up as the mechanism within Fingal County Council for "developing, co-ordinating and implementing a coherent and integrated approach to local and community development" through the implementation of the community element of a Local Economic and Community Plan for Fingal. This plan is currently being developed in 2015. The Department of Housing, Planning, Community and Local Government-funded Social Inclusion and Community Activation Programme (SICAP) is the first programme to come within the oversight of the Committee and was subject to a tendering process. The Blanchardstown Area Partnership was the successful tenderer.

RAPID, on the other hand, is an older designation led by the Department of Housing, Planning, Community and Local Government nationally. Previously, the Fingal County Development Board was the local co-ordinator for the designation, but as this body has been dissolved, responsibility for this initiative has been transferred to the Council. Through this designation, a local plan had been developed which had defined the key issues, objectives and actions that needed to be addressed locally (see Box 3.4 for a review of key issues identified in 2012). There were three local Area Implementation Team (AITs), now renamed "Task Groups": Corduff, Blakestown/Mountview, and Mulhuddart. They are being led and facilitated by a combination of the local authority (community department) and community and voluntary groups (such as Blanchardstown Area Partnership, Safer Blanchardstown, Foróige[6]).

Box 3.4. Key issues identified by the RAPID programme in 2012

An overview of the RAPID programme in 2012 raised the following issues:

- Training and Education – given the long term inter-generational unemployment which exists alongside more recent unemployment and youth unemployment there is a need to have a number of different strategies to provide information, develop and upskill the diverse range of needs.
- Integration – significant challenges exist in RAPID communities due to their increasing multicultural composition. There are substantial difficulties in meeting demands for English language classes.
- Capital Programmes – significant investment has been made in infrastructural facilities in the RAPID area and generally these are well used. However, there is a need to make sure they are maintained and sustained.
- Child and Adolescent Mental Health Service (CAMHS) – the CAMHS service will be located in a new Primary Care Centre being developed in Corduff. This Primary Care Centre will house a primary care team, GPs, a CAMHS team and an Early Intervention Team (EIT).
- Family Support – initiatives such as "Strengthening Families" have been very successful in targeting vulnerable families in Blanchardstown. There is a need to continue this work.
- Technology – communicating with people in the RAPID area through posters and leaflets needs to be supplemented with an increasing use of technology.
- Community engagement/representation – there are challenges to ensure that communities are fully engaged and represented.

Source: Bookle, S. (2012), "Final Report: Blanchardstown RAPID AIT".

However, efforts under the banner of RAPID are winding down. The AITs last met in December 2013, and have no plans to meet further. The position of the RAPID Co-Ordinator has been dissolved, and the core duties, which included facilitating inward investment and improving service integration initiatives, have been redeployed within the Council.[7] Additionally, while money was available in the first phase of the project (e.g., in 2002 to build facilities such as community centres and playgrounds), by and large, new resources are no longer allocated to RAPID areas. Since the second phase started in 2006, the focus has been on better targeting of existing resources and integrating service delivery. This has proved more difficult and is seen as a longer term project.

Finally, the Blanchardstown Area Partnership (BAP) is a key institution in tackling disadvantage in the Blanchardstown area, although since 2008 its remit has been broadened to be responsible for providing services to the whole of the Dublin 15 area. It is one of around 50 Local Development Companies operating in Ireland, and its main role is to implement programmes which support the community to identify and access opportunities for education and training, leading to progression and employment, although it also provides other services.[8]

Under a "cohesion process" BAP absorbed three community development projects from Corduff, Mulhuddart and Blakestown. However, it has retained these offices as outreach centres. The Local Employment Services, situated in Mulhuddart and Mountview, come under the Partnership's remit. Under an ongoing "alignment process" BAP will come under the auspices of Fingal County Council through the Local Community Development Committee. Under this arrangement the BAP will have to tender to provide education, training and community programmes to disadvantaged people, along with or competing against, private and other companies. Local development companies, such as BAP, could bid for SICAP programme delivery, as described above, and BAP has been awarded the contract to deliver the Social Inclusion and Community Activation Programme (SICAP) across the county of Fingal. In addition, the Department of Social Protection is introducing a new activation programme, JobPath, through tendering to private and other providers. While BAP also competed to deliver this programme, the tender has been awarded to Seetac to deliver JobPath in a number of local authorities, including Fingal, starting in 2016. Seetac is a UK-based company which provides welfare to work and skills training programmes.

Specific policy areas

Income support, employment and training

A number of institutions are involved in the field of income support, employment and training. The Blanchardstown Intreo Office is a single point of contact for all employment and income support services, a "one-stop shop" that has taken on the responsibility of a number of agencies delivering these services previously. It is located in the north-east of Blanchardstown, to the east of Corduff, and has been operational since April 2013.

With the introduction of Intreo, the emphasis has changed from a payments only service to also providing support for job seeking, through the "activation" process. When people arrive at the office for the first time they are assessed for income support. They are also invited to attend a group information session and then have a one-to-one session with a case officer. This is to obtain a profile of the person and, on this basis, to suggest education and training supports, or other options to assist them in getting a job. An agreed Personal Progression Plan is put in place. If they refuse to engage in this process there is a reduction in their payment. Experience to date has shown that very few people have had their benefits cut.

There is a wide range of options available for people – from referral to the local employment service or other Blanchardstown Area Partnership programmes, through education options such as Momentum and the Back to Education Initiative to work experience programmes such as Community Employment, Tús, JobBridge, and Gateway, the employment programme delivered through the local authorities. Linkages have also been developed with the Dublin Dun Laoghaire Education and Training Board (DDLETB), more specifically with Baldoyle Training Centre, for the referral of unemployed people to further education programmes.[9] The focus is on progression, with a view to moving people off income support. However, experience of the activation process to date, especially with those who are most disadvantaged, is that some are not familiar with the range of choices which are available, and the implications of adhering to a programme. There are challenges too for staff, particularly for those new to working with vulnerable people.

In 2015, the Blanchardstown Intreo Office focused on unemployed young people under 25, in line with the commitments in the Youth Guarantee. The activation process focuses on progression to work, which includes referring young people to training and further education. Examples of the types of activities undertaken are provided in Box 3.5.

Box 3.5. Examples of activities for young people organised by the Blanchardstown Intreo Office

Trips have been organised to local employers for young jobseekers, to give them insight into the world of work. Mock interviews have been carried out in the Intreo office, supported by local employers.

Staff from the Intreo Office have met with the CEO of the Community Training Centre, which focuses on under 18s who have dropped out of school and who are not part of the formal activation process. Work is ongoing to inform young school leavers of this initiative. The Employer Forum schools project will also work to prevent young people becoming welfare claimants, and this project will link with the Community Training Centre.

The Intreo Office has been involved in the "First Steps" programme under the Youth Guarantee, whereby host employers take on jobseekers via JobBridge, with a particular emphasis on continued employer training and mentoring. For example, Marks and Spencer is the host employer in the area which has taken on three young jobseekers via JobBridge. This initiative is being closely monitored by an Intreo case officer.

The activation process itself focuses on the skills required for future vacancies and refers young jobseekers to appropriate education or training to match this. In general, the young jobseeker would not have had work experience. During a "Jobs Week", young jobseekers were motivated to upskill or become empowered through inspirational talks. Visits were organised to the closest Training Centre in Baldoyle to give an insight into apprenticeships, and to a local employer to provide an insight into the world of work. In relation to the local employer visited, interested jobseekers could avail of warehouse training to increase their skills to obtain work in this industry.

As discussed in the previous section, the Blanchardstown Area Partnership is one of the key agencies in Blanchardstown helping the most disadvantaged integrate into the labour market, and it receives many referrals from the Intreo office. The BAP staff seek to match people's education and training needs with employers' needs. For example, young women are often trained as health care assistants, and young men for security work, as there is a demand for these types of work in the area. BAP runs several programmes, including the following:

- **Local and Community Development Programme/Social Inclusion and Community Activation Programme** – The Local and Community Development Programme was replaced with the Social Inclusion and Community Activation Programme (SICAP) in 2015. As stated above, BAP has been awarded responsibility for delivering SICAP throughout the whole of the Fingal county area. This programme provides formal and informal education and training for employment and self-employment. It supports organisations working with young people in the D15 area. Areas of work also include child and family wellbeing and support for the integration of communities.

- **Local Employment Service** – The Local Employment Service provides a mediation service for long-term unemployed men and women who wish to enter the workforce. In addition, there are a number of specific training programmes available to clients of the service, including CV preparation, interview skills, career directions, etc. There is also a Jobs Club which provides focused job preparation workshops over a period of two to three weeks. Elements of this work, specifically employment activation aimed at the long-term unemployed and those most distant from the labour market, will now be delivered through a new Department of Social Protection programme called JobPath. JobPath will be delivered in Fingal County by a UK-based company, Seetac, starting in 2016.
- **Enterprise supports** – The Enterprise Unit in the Partnership promotes self-employment, especially through the use of the Back to Work Enterprise Allowance Scheme (administered by DSP). For example, in 2011 and 2012, more than 200 businesses were established in each of these years. The demand for the service has increased since the economic crash in 2008. A survey of businesses started in 2012 found that 65% were still trading four years later (Ryan, 2014).
- **Tús programme** – The BAP also manages the Tús programme, where people are randomly selected from the Live Register to work in community organisations for 19.5 hours per week. There are 120 places on this programme, which does not include training.

Other education and training courses in the area are overseen by the Dublin Dún Laoghaire Education and Training Board (DDLETB). DDLETB is the result of a merger of County Dublin Vocational Education Committee and Dún Laoghaire Vocational Education Committee that took place in July 2013. DDLETB oversees the Blanchardstown Adult Education Service and Blanchardstown Youthreach. Blanchardstown Adult Education Service, based in Riversdale Community College, provides a wide range of courses such as adult basic education, literacy, Back to Education Initiative, Vocational Training Opportunities Scheme (VTOS), skills for work and return to learning within the north-west County Dublin area. Blanchardstown Youthreach serves 70 full-time Youthreach students and 24 part-time students under the Back to Education Initiative.

Training is also provided through the Baldoyle Training Centre, under the auspices of DDLETB, in response to specific needs identified in consultation with local DSP personnel. While not in the Blanchardstown area, the Baldoyle Training Centre provides a wide range of day and night courses for people who are unemployed in the DDLETB area.[10] Some of the courses are delivered locally if there is sufficient demand and available premises. In addition, the DDLETB provides funding for the Blanchardstown Community Training Centre. This Centre provides vocational preparation and life skills training to meet the needs of early school leavers and local young people, but only has 40 places.

The Institute of Technology Blanchardstown is located in the area for those who wish to pursue higher education. There are current proposals to merge IT Blanchardstown with IT Tallaght and Dublin IT into a Technological University with a mandate to provide education and research that is industry focused.

The Momentum initiative, administered by SOLAS and delivered through the Education and Training Board (ETB) and other local providers, and the Back to Education Initiative, delivered through the ETB, have proved popular for early school leavers and unemployed people wishing to acquire the skills to access work where there are currently job opportunities.

Despite these efforts, the very high levels of unemployment in the RAPID area suggest that existing policies are not succeeding in providing the type of transformative and personalised service that unemployed and inactive residents need. In particular, a few issues stand out as needing to be addressed.

For one, the study area is surrounded by businesses and employers, but there seems to be a disconnect in terms of people from the study area accessing the jobs available. There is some ongoing work to improve links with employers in the area, especially with regard to providing work experience for young people who have never worked before, including the establishment of an Employer Forum in 2014 (see Box 3.6) and the Youth Guarantee. In addition, employers who have engaged in the JobsPlus programme, for example, have generally found this to be a positive experience. However, overall, there is a recognised need, on the part of both the relevant public services and employers, to strengthen these links and overcome existing barriers (information provision, the rules of various employment schemes, etc.).

Box 3.6. **Blanchardstown Employer Forum**

An Employer Forum was established in Blanchardstown in 2014. The Forum, which is led by the Department of Social Protection, brings together employers and other stakeholders involved in enabling jobseekers to return to work. It comprises representatives of Blanchardstown Area Partnership, Fingal County Council, Fingal Dublin Chamber of Commerce, three small local employers, manager of the Blanchardstown Centre, Dublin and Dun Laoghaire Education and Training Board Training Centre, Baldoyle, the Blanchardstown Institute of Technology, and school liaison officer. This Forum, which meets quarterly, is working to ensure that all the opportunities for jobs, training and education are prioritised for jobseekers in Blanchardstown and its environs. The Tánaiste (deputy prime minister), who is also the Minister for Social Protection, attends meetings of the Forum.

The aim of the Forum is to help employers create jobs by giving them:

- Access to unemployed people to help fill their vacancies
- Information on employer supports, such as JobsPlus and JobBridge
- Information on employee supports, for example, Family Income Supplement, part-time work supports, afterschool childcare scheme
- Use of the Local Employment Service.

Local employers on the Forum have been involved in local endeavours, such as advice on CV preparation and mock interviews. The Department of Social Protection has delivered information sessions to retailers in the Blanchardstown Centre on the supports available to both employers and jobseekers, and held a meeting with school liaison officers with a view to addressing the "school to work gap".

As the work of the Forum evolves, employers are becoming more engaged in Intreo activation projects and have engaged with the Department of Social Protection's "Jobs Week". Events as part of Jobs Week included practical information on training, education and future skills requirements through to motivational talks by sports stars, actors and entrepreneurs.

Additionally, there are limited options available for vocational education and apprenticeships. There is no Post Leaving Certificate (PLC) centre or major training centre in the area, although there is access to PLC courses and training provided in community centres and other available premises where there is a demand. The limited availability of apprenticeships was continually raised, and it was noted that the provision of apprenticeships is under national review. It was also noted that there is an unmet demand for upskilling people who are already in jobs.

For the courses that are available, there seem to be mismatches between the demand and supply. In some cases, the demand for slots exceeds the numbers available, while in others, slots are hard to fill, often because of other barriers such as the availability or accessibility of premises (see earlier section on accessibility and spatial layout) or the lack of suitable childcare provision for those with young children.

Finally, more could be done to map the existing skills sets in Blanchardstown and assess how they might be better matched and developed to local and Dublin based employment opportunities. This could also usefully inform local careers advice.

Creating opportunities in social enterprises and other community employers

There are a number of social enterprises operating in the area, some of which provide jobs, work experience or training for local jobseekers. The Community Employment Programme, in particular, supports social enterprises in the area – for example, Base, which provides incubation units for small enterprises (many of whom avail of the Back to Work Enterprise Allowance), and Baptec, a company which provides IT training for people who are unemployed and on low incomes. The Department of Social Protection also supports a number of social enterprises in the area through the Community Service Programme in Dublin 15, to the value of around EUR 730 000 per annum.

There is also a Community Employment Programme which provides training for those who wish to work in childcare, that is, a three-year programme in "D15 Early Years Training Programme". Jobseekers can train and receive qualifications to increase their job-seeking opportunities. At the same time, they are providing affordable childcare for the community.

The Irish Sports Council is located in Blanchardstown, with a link to the Football Association of Ireland (FAI) where JobBridge is facilitated for a number of young jobseekers. In addition, the National Indoor Arena is in the progress of being built in Blanchardstown. An event was organised to promote JobsPlus and the main recruiter for this initiative has taken on a number of long-term jobseekers for general operative posts.

Migrant integration

As noted earlier, there is a large migrant population in Blanchardstown, with many immigrants in the area facing challenges integrating into Irish society. One worrying development is the high level of ethnic segregation that appears to be developing on certain housing estates, particularly in the private rented housing sector. While there are a number of national organisations providing support for migrants, such as the Immigrant Council of Ireland, the Migrant Rights Centre and the New Communities Partnership, there are few migrant organisations locally.

Some 38% of those on the Live Register in Blanchardstown are non-Irish nationals. A particular need in the area is the provision of ESOL (English for Speakers of Other Languages) classes for the large migrant population in Blanchardstown. While there is provision, such as the "Ready Steady Go European Integration Fund" (EIF) Project (see Box 3.7) delivered by the Blanchardstown Area Partnership, officially, the provision of English language classes falls under the remit of the Department of Education and Skills, through the Education and Training Boards. Recently, a Momentum provider has been recruiting candidates for English language training.

However, demand continues to outstrip supply. The response in the consultation meetings was that the language needs of migrants need to be addressed to enable them to access jobs and to ensure integration into Irish society, despite constraints to increasing provision identified by government agencies. The success of the second generation will depend on a number of factors, but these include the level of integration that their parents are able to achieve.

Box 3.7. **The Ready Steady Go European Integration Fund (EIF) project**

Blanchardstown Local Employment Service (LES), which is managed by Blanchardstown Area Partnership (BAP), receives referrals from the Blanchardstown Intreo Office, with a view to supporting their job seeking efforts and placing them on appropriate training or employment programmes. Over time, it became apparent that a high number of these referrals were "non-progression ready" due to their poor English language skills. Many of these people were "third country nationals", i.e. non-EU nationals.

In response to this demand, BAP applied under the EIF Fund to provide English language training with a focus on job skills to move "non-progression ready" clients towards the labour market. The application was successful. BAP was partnered in this endeavor by the Department of Social Protection, which contributed match funding to enable the project to go ahead. Fingal County Council also contributed match funding. This is an example of where an integrated approach can support the needs of the local community.

English language training is now provided to "third country nationals", through the EIF (along with a number of other sources of funding), in Blakestown Resource Centre.

A FETAC Level 3 course is provided. This is a six-week course for four hours per day (9.30am to 1.30pm, Monday to Friday). Five weeks are spent on learning English and one week on job seeking. To date, three courses have been provided with positive outcomes.

Learning from the provision of these courses is the need to acknowledge low levels of literacy in some cases (a pre-FETAC course may be required) and cultural issues in relation to how education and training is provided. For example, there is a requirement for those on the course to attend every day and to arrive on time.

Drugs and crime

Drugs and community safety programmes are delivered through the Blanchardstown Local Drugs Taskforce and Safer Blanchardstown. The Local Drugs Taskforce was set up in Blanchardstown by the government over a decade ago to tackle the drugs problem in the area. The aim of the local drugs task force is to work collaboratively with the local community, voluntary groups and the state sector in assessing the extent and nature of the drug problem in the area and then to co-ordinate action at local level so that there is a targeted response to the drug problem in local communities. The task force implements the National Drugs Strategy in the context of the needs of the area, through action plans on supply reduction; prevention; treatment; rehabilitation; and research. The Blanchardstown local drugs task force is based in Mulhuddart, also covering Corduff, with local drugs teams in Mountview/Blakestown and Huntstown/Hartstown. The Local Drugs Task Force is currently in a state of flux as its funding has been reduced over a five-year period, and there is some uncertainty about how it will operate in the future.

Safer Blanchardstown is the Local Community Policing Forum set up under the Garda Síochána Act 2005 (Irish Police Force). It works in the same areas as the Local Drugs Task Force, i.e. Corduff, Mulhuddart, Blakestown, Mountview, Hartstown and Huntstown. Safer Blanchardstown aims, through a partnership approach, to increase communication, trust and relevant information exchange between local residents and the appropriate authorities. The forum also aims to ensure that all residents have an opportunity to take part in shaping policing priorities for their area in order to help tackle issues of crime, drug dealing, anti-social behaviour and other criminal activity.

Safer Blanchardstown reports twice annually to the Fingal Joint Policing Committee. This committee is a partnership between Fingal County Council, An Garda Síochána and the community. The purpose of the Fingal Joint Policing Committee is to provide a forum where the County Council and senior Garda officers, together with elected representatives and community interests, can meet and consider matters which affect the policing of the county, e.g. public order, anti-social behaviour and general community safety issues. This provides an opportunity for the various participants to engage in finding a solution and making recommendations to the Committee on the issues raised.

The ability of the various programmes delivered through such initiatives to adequately address the drugs and crime problems in the area remains an ongoing debate. For instance, some community personnel are of the view that drug debt intimidation has become a growing concern across Drugs Task Force areas. It is viewed as a continuum of behaviour from mild to severe to ruthless. Rather than focus merely on the perpetrators and victims, there is a need to explore the root causes and how people became either victims or perpetrators and to see the issue as being ordered along a continuum from lower order (8 to 16 year olds who break windows, damage cars, and have little to no parental direction) to middle order (13 to 20 year olds who use drugs, carry out drug-related crime and anti-social behaviour) through to higher order (17 year olds and over who are drug dealers, part of drug gangs and may be involved in gun crime) (Jennings, 2013).

Public officials, however, are of the view that there is no longer a significant drug problem in the area, and that the Gardaí (police force) has responded to the issue of drug-related intimidation. This response involves: having a single point of contact; ensuring a confidential, safe and effective means of dealing with reports of intimidation; and providing families with sufficient support from the Gardaí. The National Family Support Network, in partnership with the Garda National Drugs Unit, and other key agencies, has developed a drug-related intimidation reporting programme leaflet and a "responding to intimidation" video as well as providing contact details for nominated "Inspectors for Intimidation Programme".

While the spatial layout of housing estates and open spaces has been acknowledged to play a role in making the area vulnerable to crime (e.g. by the Local Drugs Task Force, the Dublin Institute of Technology and the RAPID co-ordinator amongst others – see McCulloch et al., 2010), this has only fed weakly into policy actions up until now. Fingal County Council, for example, conducted building alterations in one particular drug and crime hotspot so that the houses faced outwards into the surrounding urban area, as opposed to inwards into a less supervised public space. Before, the semi-private courtyard had provided a space for criminal activity that was unwatched by local passers-by.

Family and children's services

Given the young age profile of the area it is worth mentioning the Family Resource Centre (FRC) in Whitechapel, Mountview which provides education and training supports, counselling services, childcare facilities and parenting support. For example, the Parent Plus Early Years Programme is run out of Mountview FRC. It is a seven-week course for parents of pre-schoolers and young children. The programme supports parents to help their children communicate and learn in play, to manage difficult behaviour, to creatively help their children to learn and to develop good relationships with their children.

Within the RAPID area there are nine childcare facilities. Five of these are provided by community organisations and four are private. In addition, the Department of Social Protection facilitates access to affordable after school childcare for those on JobBridge and for those returning to work. A number of youth organisations cater to the needs of young people in the area. An aspect of this is a Youth Employment Initiative, funded by the European Social Fund, which is delivered by the Blanchardstown Area Partnership and Foróige, the national youth development organisation.

The need to improve access to services for children and families in the study area was raised at the roundtable discussions, particularly in relation to childcare and early education, including the need for supports for providers to meet the required standards. Additionally, it was stated that services need to interact with families in a more integrated way. For instance, in some cases, a number of services may be engaging on an individual, siloed basis with a family. It was felt that, in such circumstances, a more holistic and integrated response would be more beneficial in supporting the family to progress and improve their situation.

Health and mental health

Health issues, especially mental health issues, were evident in the study area. These included stress, anger management, family issues, anxiety, depression and suicide. There is also a recognised need to acknowledge the role of carers of people with ill health or disabilities and the supports which are available for them, including respite care. It was also noted that acknowledgement of having mental health issues can be stigmatising and make people reluctant to be seen to be accessing such services.

In terms of services available, a Child and Adolescent Mental Health Service (CAMHS) will be provided in the new Primary Care Centre in Corduff, which will also house a primary care team, GPs and an Early Intervention Team. An organisation, Jigsaw Dublin 15 (a project of Headstrong, The National Centre for Youth Mental Health) also provides a service for young people with mental health issues, see Box 3.8.

Box 3.8. Jigsaw Dublin 15 – a mental health service for young people in Blanchardstown

Jigsaw provides a free, confidential, one-to-one mental health support service for young people along with Mental Health Training and Awareness in the community. Jigsaw is funded and supported by private and state sources.

Jigsaw Dublin 15, located in the public library building in Blanchardstown, is one of 10 Jigsaw projects throughout the country. It is a discreet, warm and friendly service and environment. Young people are involved in every stage of the design and delivery of the mental health supports through a Youth Advisory Panel (YAP).

Jigsaw Dublin 15 was set up in 2012, following extensive consultation and pre-development work. A number of levels of governance, involving a wide range of stakeholders, oversee the work of Jigsaw Dublin 15. The service Jigsaw Dublin 15 provides is in a non-clinical and youth-friendly environment, and by maintaining a brief, early intervention model, waiting lists are avoided. Jigsaw Dublin 15 draws on employment support schemes, such as Tús and JobBridge, to support some elements of the work.

Evaluations of the service have shown that young people and their families feel comfortable and safe using Jigsaw Dublin 15. Young people learn skills such as when to seek help, how to solve problems and how to cope in various situations. Where required, people are connected to more specialised services.

Cross-cutting challenges

A number of issues that cross-cut the specific policy areas create challenges for effectively tackling disadvantage and promoting inclusive growth in Blanchardstown. For example, many of the central government delivered policies are being implemented in their standard form in Blanchardstown. There appear to be some gaps that have emerged, especially in meeting the needs of new migrant communities and the long term unemployed. Overall, despite the creation of Intreo, there appears to be a lack of an integrated approach built around the individual that is able to be flexible enough to meet individual needs. Intreo takes an important step in this direction, but as it is focused specifically on employment, there is room for this approach to be further enhanced and broadened. These cross-cutting challenges, and others, are discussed in more detail below.

National policies are having unintended consequences locally

Some aspects of the impact of national policy at the local level have been highlighted in the previous section. Some of the most pertinent issues are related to land use zoning, planning and housing policy. These are designed at a wider national or regional level and have compounded many of the issues of disadvantage in the RAPID area of Blanchardstown, e.g. concentrations of migrants, lone parents, and unemployed people in certain estates, limited accessibility to amenities in some of the estates, and issues of community safety.

A lack of flexibility in key policies also impedes stakeholders in addressing specific local needs. This is particularly relevant to Blanchardstown because its population is far more diverse than the rest of Ireland, especially in relation to the proportion of ethnic minorities, which have different needs from the native Irish population, e.g. in relation to language issues, health needs, as well as recognition of cultural values.

Fragmentation in service delivery leads to disjointed pathways, overlaps and gaps

Because of the way national policies are delivered at local level, compounded by an environment of institutional and policy change, lines of implementation and accountability are often vertical, so that delivery at the local level can be fragmented, with gaps in provision and disrupted pathways between services.

At the moment, there also seems to be some uncertainty in who is responsible for what at the local level. Local stakeholders noted that there was no structured forum for learning about the work that the various statutory, voluntary and community organisations were undertaking or meaningful mechanisms for horizontal accountability. This has several repercussions. For example, at the roundtables it was noted that, "hard-to-reach" may actually be a misnomer for the most disadvantaged families. In fact, many of these families are being served by multiple agencies but not in a way that is strategic or co-ordinated. Additionally, issues as simple as timing – e.g. large delays between when one education/training programme ends and the next in a progressive pathway starts – can impede people's transitions between services. Some stakeholders felt that, as a result of this fragmentation, services are focused too much on addressing the symptoms of disadvantage, rather than the root causes.

Examples of where this currently operates, and has the potential to better co-ordinate services at the local level, is through the County Childcare Committee and Children and Young People's Services Committee. The Fingal County Childcare Committee supports a range of training programmes and workshops. These relate to childcare providers, childminders and parents. The Committee's over-riding role is to act in an advisory capacity to support and assist childcare practitioners and families in Fingal County. Fingal Children and Young People's Services Committee is a county-wide, inter-agency group whose role is to improve outcomes for children in Fingal. Its remit is to bring services together to work more collaboratively, avoid duplication and address gaps. A challenge for services in the Blanchardstown RAPID area is to ensure sufficient focus and resources to meet the identified level of need within the broader county-wide framework.

The "scaling" of interventions is compounding Blanchardstown's challenges

As identified above, one of the key policy challenges in Blanchardstown is getting the scale of policy interventions right. Overall, for an urban area of this size, it appears that Blanchardstown suffers from a lack of appropriate governance at both local level and as part of its city region. For local issues it is managed from county level, and the area is split between two municipal districts. Its spatial incoherence is evidenced by the way in which most national agencies respond to the area through an area definition based on its postcode of D15. At the regional level, there is a need to better take into account its role within the Greater Dublin functional urban area as a residential location, and as a site of large employers. Many of the problems of Blanchardstown's growth in the past two decades can only be addressed by a coherent approach at city-regional level. This applies to decisions on inward investment and improving access to the labour market for Blanchardstown residents.

One potential manifestation of this challenge is the LCDC. As it currently stands, the LCDC operates at the county level, and it remains to be seen whether this will impede its ability to create meaningful change in a targeted area such as Blanchardstown. Potential strategies for addressing this challenge could include the operation of more than one LCDC for the county (as allowed by the 2014 Local Government Act with permission from the Minister) or the development of a sub-group for the area of Blanchardstown.

A related challenge is that many organisational and administrative boundaries are not co-terminus, for example, Blanchardstown is split between two electoral areas (Castleknock and Mulhuddart) as noted earlier. When boundaries are not aligned it can be difficult for organisations to collaborate and to target resources where they are most needed. It would be useful to identify agreed administrative boundaries and collect data at this level, which can subsequently be aggregated to meet the needs of particular organisations.

Recent reforms have potential for positive change, but will need to be implemented carefully

In the context of the recent reforms, a clear issue for the Fingal LCDC, and LCDCs in general, is their capacity to address the issues of disadvantage which exist in areas like Blanchardstown. Effective implementation of LCDCs will require not only technical expertise, but also strong networking and inter-personal skills. A related factor is that many of the services to be provided in disadvantaged areas through the LCDC will be tendered to private companies and/or community organisations. For example, in Blanchardstown the SICAP was awarded to Blanchardstown Area Partnership following a tendering process. In general, in adopting a tendering approach care will need to be taken to ensure that a competitive environment does not jeopardise collaborative working, disperse scarce resources too thinly or create perverse delivery incentives. Oversight by the LCDC of the SICAP programme is intended to lessen these risks. Informal networking is also an important component of co-ordinating service provision at the local level. However, with institutional change and staff turnover, many of these networks have been disrupted. Opportunities to re-connect and build new working relationships will be important in ensuring better co-ordination of local services in the future.

Community assets are not yet leveraged to their full potential

Finally, the existing assets of the community are not yet being fully leveraged, and further heavy lifting is needed on the part of both national and local actors to make better use of the assets that already exist in the community. For example, efforts are already being made to link local residents to local employers, but these could be further strengthened.

Social enterprises are now playing a more important role in helping galvanise positive links between local people, employers and service providers, thanks to the support that they are receiving locally. Social enterprises in Blanchardstown are relevant to help the local council to target the population's needs. Local policy makers' action to consolidate social enterprises by financially supporting their initial development and by facilitating their access to the local market is an important strategy which should be continued.

There are also several international examples of how social enterprises can work with migrant communities, which could be relevant in Blanchardstown (see Box 3.9). In Sweden, one such initiative has been successful in reaching out to migrant communities, while also providing employment opportunities. Based on positive results, a franchising model has been created and a number of local authorities are replicating the partnership with the social enterprise. In Blanchardstown, social enterprises could usefully complement the efforts of the Ready Steady Go project (see Box 3.7) that is providing linguistic training to immigrant residents. The South Tyrone Empowerment Programme (STEP) has another interesting approach. STEP provides one-to-one advice on a range of migrant issues, runs an interpretation service and also does community development work around common issues. The situation in Northern Ireland is helped by the existence of equality legislation, originally introduced in the context of the Troubles, but now helping all communities in Northern Ireland to improve access to services.

Conclusion

While Blanchardstown is a community with a number of assets – e.g. large number of employers, high levels of infrastructure investment, strong community spirit – it continues to struggle with high rates of unemployment and social exclusion. Two key factors help to explain this situation. Firstly, many of the positive benefits associated with the assets in Blanchardstown do not reach the people who actually live there. For example, community residents are not able to access jobs at many of the large, multi-national employers that are located in the community. The shopping centre and the business park have been planned with convenient access to motorways, allowing large-scale regional access, but do not form an accessible local core. In other words, despite the efforts underway, much of Blanchardstown's assets currently benefit other communities, rather than Blanchardstown itself. Secondly, Blanchardstown has to deal with the negative ramifications of many of the decisions made regionally or nationally which have a disproportionate impact on the area. Many national or regional challenges are "parked" in Blanchardstown, from migrant integration to addressing social exclusion on housing estates.

Thus, addressing these challenges will require action across governance levels. At the local level, existing efforts to strategically leverage community assets, as well as to better co-ordinate services, could be further enhanced. At the national and regional levels, more consideration is needed on how to minimise unintentional impacts that decisions taken at higher levels can have on places like Blanchardstown. While the recent local governance reforms hold promise, overall, "heavier lifting" on the part of both national and local actors is needed to bring in the resources and capacities that Blanchardstown requires to get to the roots of many challenges it is facing.

Box 3.9. Examples of social enterprises involved in migrant integration

Macken, Växjö, Sweden. Macken is a social enterprise created in 2004 as a recycling business in Växjö, a town in southern Sweden with a foreign-born population of 14%, over half of whom are unemployed. One of the barriers to the integration of migrants is their poor command of Swedish. Macken therefore had the idea of offering practice-oriented language training to its workers. It contacted the National Centre for Swedish as a Second Language, which referred them to a Danish model of practice-based language learning. Macken developed a methodology, and the municipal council agreed to purchase trainee places in its "language workshops". Macken has since opened an enterprise centre, a business school and an agricultural college. Numerous other local authorities showed interest in Macken's experience, and with support from Explosion, an ESF project managed by Companion (a network supporting the development of co-operatives) in Göteborg, it developed a social franchising model. The first franchise opened in Högsby in August 2013 and others are under development.

STEP, Dungannon, Northern Ireland. STEP, or South Tyrone Empowerment Programme, is a social enterprise operating in Dungannon in Northern Ireland. From 2000, Dungannon experienced the fastest growth in population of any part of Northern Ireland, largely driven by a rapid growth in migrants, initially from Portugal, Cape Verde and East Timor and after EU enlargement from Poland, and to a lesser extent from the Czech Republic, Hungary and the Baltic states. The organisation adapted its operations to meet the needs of these new groups and set up a number of new services including:

- One-to-one advice provided by bilingual advice workers.
- Legal aid for more complex cases – especially focusing on immigration, and employment rights.
- Community development, social capital and community cohesion in neighbourhoods – working with resident groups to counter racist attacks, developing social activities and language clubs.
- Research and policy on migrant communities and responding to consultations - through a dedicated research officer working on the needs of local communities and publishing results, as well as contributing to larger studies.
- Interpretation and translation services – provided through a wholly owned social enterprise subsidiary Step Training Limited (STL).
- Training and accreditation.

STEP adopts a human rights-based approach to its work with government agencies and communities and has a strong values-based approach. The programme's use of advisers from within the communities has enabled it to overcome language difficulties. It provides training and accreditation for advisers and interpreters.

By 2012, when the last evaluation was carried out, the STEP group was employing 28 people in three locations and had established a separate law centre service. It had also established revenue - generating social enterprise, Step Training Limited (STL), which cross-subsidised the parent organisation and provides up to 40% of STEP's resources. It makes a surplus on training, property management and interpretation. Over 50 self-employed interpreters have been trained by STL and are booked by them to deliver interpretation services to public bodies operating in health, education, housing, employment and welfare. Other income included a grant from Atlantic Philanthropies, EU transnational projects, and national funds.

Source: Social Entrepreneurship Network (n.d.), "Policy meets practice. Enabling the growth of social enterprises", 2013-14, http://socialeconomy.pl/sites/default/files/files/Social%20Entrepreneurship%20Network_final_Publication.pdf.

Notes

1. RAPID was a focused government initiative to target the 51 most disadvantaged areas and provincial areas in the country. RAPID aimed to bring about significant improvements in the lives of the residents of its communities through: improving the delivery of public services through integration and co-ordination; improving opportunities for communities to participate in the strategic improvement of their areas; and giving priority access to available resources to RAPID communities. RAPID was implemented locally by a cross-sectoral Area Implementation Team which included representatives of the community, relevant state agencies and other partners. It was supported by a RAPID co-ordinator. Although the programme is no longer funded, the RAPID area boundaries are still in existence. Future RAPID implementation arrangements will be taken forward in the context of the local government reform programme.
2. Many of the statistics available at this level of disaggregation are from the latest Census, which was undertaken in 2011.
3. The Live Register is not designed to measure unemployment. It includes part-time workers (those who work up to three days a week), seasonal and casual workers entitled to Jobseeker's Benefit (JB) or Jobseeker's Allowance (JA). Unemployment is generally measured by the Quarterly National Household Survey using the International Labour Office (ILO) methodology or by Principal Economic Status (PES) methodology based on the Census of Population. The ILO approach is generally considered the most robust and is used in making international comparisons. However, as it is based on a household survey, data are not available at the level of D15. Thus, Live Register information is used to supplement the somewhat dated Census information.
4. For example, at national level employment overall increased by 2.9% over the last year from Q3 2014 to Q3 2015. The largest rates of increase were recorded in the construction (+13.3%) and the industry (+5.7%) sectors. In the Dublin region as a whole employment increased by 5% between Q3 2014 and Q3 2015 (Central Statistics Office, 2015b).
5. A Rent Supplement payment is designed to supplement a person's income to meet their accommodation need. There are rent limits set in legislation for each area. A claimant is expected to source their own accommodation within these limits and, subject to a means assessment, a rent supplement may be payable. This is usually paid directly to the claimant, who is also expected to make a set contribution to the rent payable. Contributions are also payable from liable relatives e.g. son/daughter on welfare/working.
6. Foróige is a national youth development organisation.
7. The previous RAPID Co-ordinator is now the LCDC Chief Officer in Fingal County Council.
8. Only the main organisations taking an area-based approach to community development have been described here. There are also other organisations in the area, such as the Blanchardstown Travellers Development Group, and youth organisations, who play an important role in supporting their respective communities.
9. The three Department of Social Protection Dublin Divisions have developed a protocol with their local Education and Training Boards. This protocol is being used as a template for a national agreement.
10. Within the DDLETB area there are also Training Centres in Loughlinstown and Tallaght.

Chapter 4

North County Meath, Ireland: Case study on social inclusion in a rural area

This chapter examines north County Meath as a case study on social inclusion in rural areas in Ireland. North County Meath is characterised by a relatively high age dependency ratio, a high number of one-person households, and a predominantly Irish population. This chapter begins by providing an overview of the social and economic context for the area. Following a discussion of the current policy framework in place to improve social inclusion, it identifies a number of overarching issues that impede efforts to improve social inclusion.

Background

The rural study area is situated in north County Meath, which is the second largest county in Leinster (Meath County Council, undated). Meath adjoins Dublin to the south, and the southern part of the county is seen as being part of the Greater Dublin Area.

Figure 4.1. **Rural case study area in context**

CASE STUDY AREA:
North County Meath
Population: 2 776
It comprises the Electoral Divisions (EDs) of Drumcondra, Kilmainham, Ardagh and Carrickleck. It is bounded by the village of Nobber to the south and the town of Kingscourt in Cavan to the north.

Kells Municipal District
Population: 28 608
Kells is one of six municipal districts in Meath which are delineated on the basis of population size. The study area falls within Kells municipal district which covers the whole north of the county and contains a dispersed rural population and a number of villages.

County Meath
Population: 184 000
Meath has the seventh highest population of all local authorities in Ireland. In the five years between 2006 and 2011 Meath experienced the fifth highest rate of population growth in Ireland. Much of this growth took place in the southern part of the county. The county has a diverse range of landscapes, with a small area of coastline to the east, drumlins to the north and extensive areas of farmland. The county includes Tara which was the ancient capital of Ireland, and also megalithic sites at Newgrange and Oldcastle, Norman castle ruins at Trim and contains the Boyne river valley. Meath has a productive agriculture and food sector, as well as being a tourist destination for historical, cultural and other sites.

The largest urban centre in north Meath is Kells, which is 20 to 25 kilometres south-west of the study area. The study area falls within the Kells Municipal District, and is bounded by three counties: Louth, Monaghan and Cavan (which all border Northern Ireland). It has links with towns in these counties for employment and services, such as Ardee, Dundalk and Drogheda in Louth, Carrickmacross in Monaghan and Kingscourt and Bailieborough in Cavan. There are two villages in the study area: Drumconrath and Kilmainhamwood. There are a total of 2 776 people enumerated in the study area, with 682 being recorded as living in the two villages. The remaining 2 094 people live in the surrounding countryside.

Drumconrath is a small historic village situated in the east of the study area and has close links to County Louth. There has been a settlement here since before 200BC. The village is set in forested drumlin countryside and is surrounded by small lakes, making it an established angling centre. The village offers a number of services, such as a primary school and some shops. There are two housing estates bordering the village, De Valera Park on the road to Nobber and Hillside View on the road to Carrickmacross. The former was built in the early 1970s and the latter during the Celtic Tiger era (late 1990s/early 2000s). There is a large community centre in the village, two churches, a Gaelic football club and a pitch and putt course. There is a small industrial estate.

Kilmainhamwood is a village and townland in the west of the study area. The village has one primary school, a church, and a Gaelic football club. In recent years a retirement village and a convalescent home have been built on a road into the village.

The following sections present the economic profile of the study area based on the profiles of the four EDs of Drumcondra, Kilmainham, Ardagh and Carrickleck. Where relevant, statistics are presented for the villages of Drumconrath and Kilmainham. County-level statistics are also presented as a point of comparison.

Demographics[1]

Relatively high age dependency ratio[2]

The age dependency rate for the study area is 54.3, which is higher than both the average for County Meath (51.7) and the state (49.3). Kilmainham has a notably high age dependency ratio of 112.2 reflecting the location of the retirement village there, with an old age dependency rate of 60.5. This compares with an old age dependency rate of 23 for the study area in general, and 16.8 in Drumconrath. The old age dependency rate for County Meath as a whole is 13.4.

County Meath overall has a relatively youthful population with a young dependency ratio of 38.3. This young population is not reflected in the study area to the same extent, where the young dependency ratio is 31.3. The young dependency rate is 27.7 in Drumconrath, but also a surprising 51.7 in Kilmainhamwood. In Kilmainhamwood this ratio reflects the low proportion of the working age population (47%) as much as a high population of young people (24%), with 29% of the population over the age of 65.

High number of one person households

When household type is considered (see Figure 4.2), the study area has a greater proportion of one-person households than the county in general. This is influenced to some extent by the high proportion of single person households in Kilmainhamwood with its large elderly population, although the proportion of single person households is also comparatively high in Drumconrath. There are fewer couples with children in Drumconrath and especially Kilmainhamwood, with the study area in general having a slightly smaller proportion than the county overall. The proportion of lone parents, however, at 16% in both Drumconrath and Kilmainhamwood, is higher than the 10% in both the study area and County Meath generally.

Predominantly Irish population

The population of the study area is predominantly Irish at 96%, compared to 88% for the county as a whole. There is a small population of UK nationals in the study area (2%) and a few (1%) eastern Europeans, predominantly Polish. There is a small Irish Traveller population, mainly in the Kilmainhamwood area.

Figure 4.2. **Household type, County Meath, 2011**

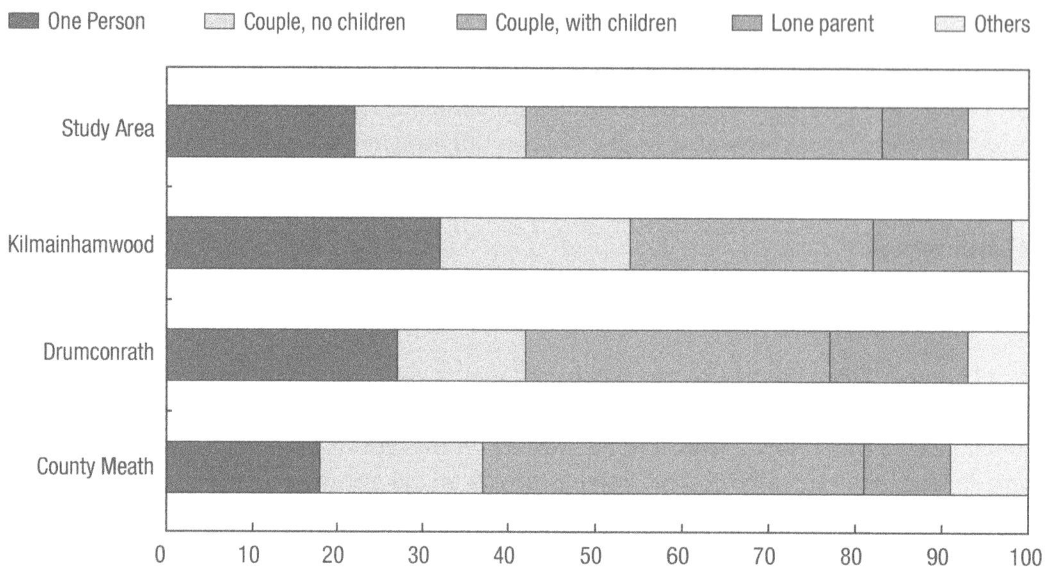

Source: CSO Census 2011 Small Area Population Statistics (SAP) at http://census.cso.ie/sapmap/

Local economy and labour market

Relatively low labour force participation rates

In 2011, the labour force participation rate for the study area as a whole was 58.3%, well below the participation rate for the county (65.8%). There is variation within the study area with the labour force participation rate in Drumconrath at 62.5%, just above the national average, while the rate for Kilmainhamwood was just 41.5% (reflecting the influence of the retirement village). At this level of disaggregation the 2011 Census figures are the most recent available. However, as noted earlier, the employment and labour market participation rates have been improving at national level since 2012, and it would be expected that there would be some improvement in the north County Meath area. Nevertheless, the extent of this improvement cannot be quantified with the data currently available.

County Meath's overall labour force participation rate was 65.8%, higher than the state average of 61.9% in 2011. Meath had the second highest labour force participation rate in the country, with only Fingal having a higher rate at 68.4% (the county within which Blanchardstown is located). An urban/rural contrast is evident, with some of the more rural and peripheral parts of the county having labour force participation rates well below the national average (van Egeraat & Gleeson, 2013).

It is noted that between 2006 and 2011 the labour force participation rate in Meath declined from 67.3%, a trend which was observed across the country. At the same time, the labour force increased by 8%, along with an increase of 15% in the non-labour force (students, looking after home/family, retired, unable to work due to sickness or disability).

Turning to non-participation in the labour market, Figure 4.3 shows the principal economic status of the population aged 15 and over in 2011 for County Meath as a whole, the study area and the two villages in the study area. As expected, Kilmainhamwood had a high proportion of the population who are retired (31%) or unable to work due to permanent sickness or disability (9%) compared to the average for the county as a whole at 10% and 4% respectively. These trends are reflected in the non-participation profile for the study area as a whole compared to County Meath, with fewer at work, a higher level of unemployment, and higher percentages of those who are retired or not able to work because they are sick or disabled. There was a comparatively small proportion of students in Drumconrath and Kilmainhamwood at 7% and 6%, compared to a county and study area average of 10%. The proportion of unemployed people was also notable in Drumconrath, as discussed below.

Figure 4.3. **Population aged 15+ by principal economic status, County Meath, 2011**

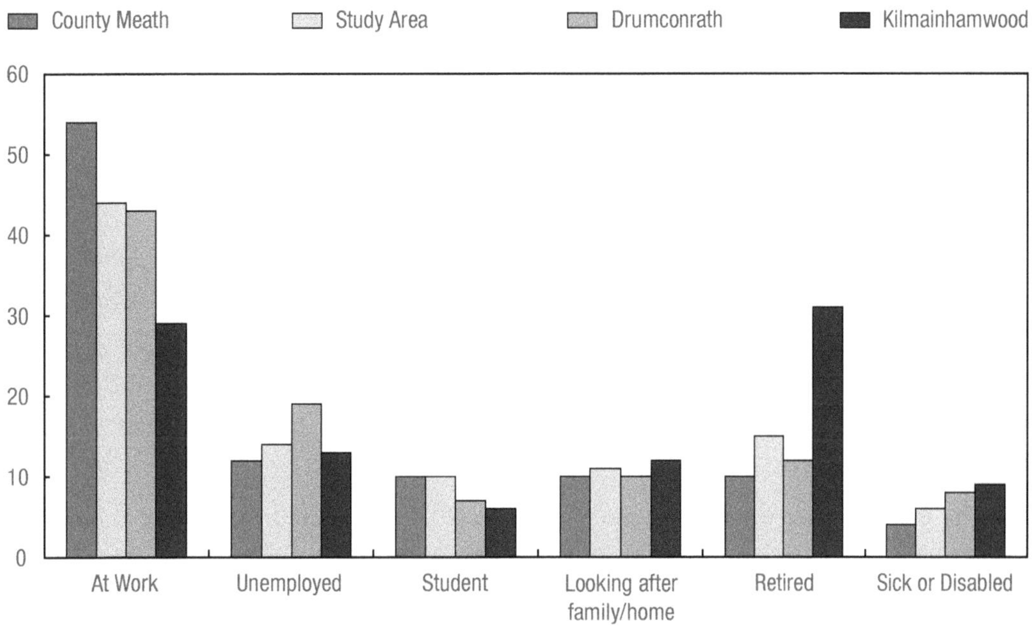

Source: CSO Census 2011 Small Area Population Statistics (SAP) at http://census.cso.ie/sapmap/

High unemployment rates, with variation by location

The study area as a whole had an unemployment rate of 25% in 2011[3], with the villages of Drumconrath and Kilmainhamwood both having much higher unemployment rates of 31%. The male unemployment rate in the study area, at 28%, was higher than the female unemployment rate of 22%. The level of unemployment in County Meath overall in 2011 was 18%, increasing from 6.5% in 2006. A clear spatial pattern of unemployment is evident across the county, with lower levels of unemployment (less than 15%) mainly in the east and south of the county. There are much higher unemployment rates in the north and west of the county with six of Meath's 92 Electoral Divisions having unemployment rates in excess of 25%. Even though the situation is expected to have improved across the county in recent years, it is not known to what extent this gap may have narrowed, if at all.

Industries vary across the county, with particularly high rates of agriculture in the study area

Figure 4.4 shows persons at work by industry in County Meath, the study area, and in the villages of Drumconrath and Kilmainhamwood in 2011.

Figure 4.4. **Workers by industry, County Meath, 2011**

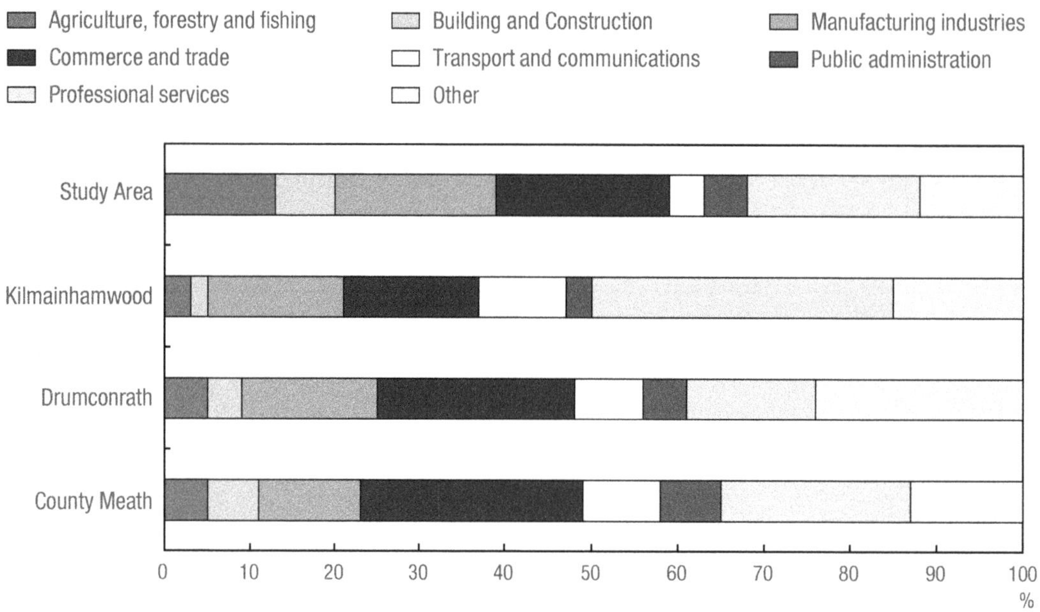

Source: CSO Census 2011 Small Area Population Statistics (SAP) at http://census.cso.ie/sapmap/

The main industries in the study area in 2011 were commerce and trade, and professional services, (both 20%) along with manufacturing services at 19%. As might be expected, agriculture, fisheries and food industries also featured strongly at 13%, along with other service activities at 12%. It is notable that building and construction was low at 7%, although this would be expected to have increased in recent years.

The main industries in the village of Drumconrath were other service activities[4] (24%) and commerce and trade (23%) followed by manufacturing industries (16%) and professional services (15%). The industry profile of Kilmainhamwood is influenced by employment in the retirement village with 35% engaged in professional services. 16% are employed in both manufacturing industries and commerce and trade, with 15% in other service activities.

In addition to the retirement village in Kilmainhamwood being a source of employment, there are a number of manufacturing industries in nearby Kingscourt, including Gypsum Industries who make plasterboards and plasters and Kingspan who make insulated panels and other insulation. Another employer, Kingscourt Brick, has recently closed.

In County Meath as a whole the main industry sectors in 2011 were commerce and trade (26%) and professional services (22%), followed by other service activities (13%) and manufacturing industries (12%). Commerce and trade and professional service workers tend to be located predominately in the south and east of the county, especially near the M1 and M3 corridors and around the main urban centres, while manufacturing and other services are more evenly distributed with manufacturing, in particular, being more heavily distributed in the north and west of the county. This is reflected in the industry profile for the study area where manufacturing services made up 19% of workers.

Most job opportunities outside of area and require a car

The majority of people in the study area travel outside the area for employment, to places like Kingscourt, Carrickmacross, Bailieborough, Kells, Ardee, as well as further to urban centres such as Navan, and Dundalk, and possibly Dublin.[5] However, the latter is a long commute of about 90 kilometres, taking nearly one and a half hours by car or two and a half hours by bus.

A car is often seen as a necessity for work in rural areas. In the study area, 10% of households did not have a car, the same as for County Meath as a whole. In the relatively remote villages of Drumconrath and Kilmainhamwood this figure rose to 18% and 17% respectively. While more than half (54%) of households in the study area had two or more cars, similar to County Meath as a whole, the comparative figures for the villages of Drumconrath and Kilmainhamwood were 41% and 31% respectively. 36% of households in the study area had one car, with comparative figures for Drumconrath and Kilmainhamwood being 41% and 52%.

Of the jobs which are available in the study area, many are part-time, and/or low paid. The challenge of providing well-paid jobs in the area was highlighted by a community childcare provider. Wages for childcare staff are somewhat of a complex issue – if wages are relatively high, the cost of the childcare is prohibitive for those who require it; but if the childcare is to be affordable for local parents, then childcare workers are paid a relatively low wage, and with limited career progression within the facility.

Relatively low levels of educational attainment

In terms of educational attainment, 21% of the population in the study area had primary education only, compared to a national average of 16%, indicating a comparatively low level of education (2011 figures). The proportions with low levels of education were even higher in the two villages, with 23% of those living in Drumconrath having primary education only, and 30% in Kilmainhamwood having only this level of education. In relation to higher qualifications, 16% of those living in the study area had third level qualifications, which was only half the national average of 31%. Even fewer had third level qualifications or higher in the two villages, with 15% in Drumconrath stating they had this level of qualification and only 10% in Kilmainhamwood qualified to this level. These statistics, to some extent, reflect the age profile of the area, and also that people with qualifications often leave the area for jobs elsewhere.

Social exclusion and deprivation

The study area in north County Meath is one of the most disadvantaged areas of the county. The Pobal HP Deprivation Index, using data from the 2011 Census, shows the overall level of deprivation and affluence in County Meath. Meath was the ninth most affluent local authority in the country, slipping from sixth in 2006. Meath experienced a very significant decline over the five-year inter-censual period, as a result of the economic downturn. Rates of deprivation vary across the county "but, in general, the county does not have any areas in the extremes of either disadvantage or affluence" (van Egeraat & Gleeson, 2013: 9). The vast majority of EDs are in the categories just above or below the average with 37% classified as marginally above average, 61% classed as marginally below average and just 2% classed as disadvantaged. One of these is Kilmainham ED, which is in the study area, and the other is Kells Urban.

Table 4.1 shows the relative deprivation of the study area in north County Meath. Overall, the area has a deprivation score of -8.26, with most of the area being marginally below average. The least deprived part of the study area is in Drumcondra ED with a deprivation score of -2.6, and the most disadvantaged is in Kilmainham ED at -18.20. Part of the Ardagh ED is also classified as disadvantaged.[6]

Table 4.1. **Areas of relative affluence and deprivation in north County Meath, 2006-2011**

Small Area	2011	2006	Change in Relative Index Score 2006-2011	Relative Deprivation Score 2011
Ardagh	-4.70	-0.60	-4.10	Marginally below average
Ardagh	-13.60	-14.10	0.50	Disadvantaged
Ardagh	-6.30	-0.60	-5.70	Marginally below average
Carrickleck	-6.50	-5.00	-1.50	Marginally below average
Carrickleck	-7.20	-1.80	-5.40	Marginally below average
Drumcondra	-4.30	1.10	-5.40	Marginally below average
Drumcondra	-6.10	-4.20	-1.90	Marginally below average
Drumcondra	-10.90	-9.90	-1.00	Disadvantaged
Drumcondra	-8.60	-2.40	-6.20	Marginally below average
Drumcondra	-2.60	-9.90	7.30	Marginally below average
Kilmainham	-18.20	-5.90	-12.30	Disadvantaged
Kilmainham	-10.60	-8.00	-2.60	Disadvantaged
TOTAL	**-8.26**	**-4.49**	**-3.77**	**Marginally below average**

Source: Haase and Pratschke (2012), "The 2011 Pobal HP Deprivation Index for Small Areas (SA)".

Low rates of computer ownership and broadband access

Another significant issue is the poor mobile phone and broadband coverage. Based on 2011 Census data the penetration of household computers and broadband was lower in the study area at 65% and 51% respectively, compared to the county as a whole where 78% of households had a personal computer and 67% had broadband access to the internet. The proportions were lower in the villages of Drumconrath and Kilmainhamwood, where just under 60% of the population had a personal computer, while 55% had broadband access to the internet in Drumconrath, but less than half (49%) did in Kilmainhamwood.

This is affecting all aspects of life for people living there. For example, it limits the farming population in accessing schemes and grants which are available on-line; it limits opportunities for businesses that operate through the internet; it limits access to on-line education and training schemes; and it limits access to on-line shopping or social activities, including interaction with family members who may be no longer living in the study area.

Isolation associated with family fragmentation, old age and poverty

North County Meath has experienced a fragmentation and dissolution of family ties in recent years, due to problems associated with the inheritance of family farms, difficulties for young people in accessing planning permission to build locally, and emigration of young people out of the area for education and work. This has resulted in a loss of social capital and problems of isolation, particularly for the elderly. Old age, poverty and loneliness are significant issues in the area, creating challenges for families, community groups and service providers such as the health service. This is compounded by the fact that as people leave the area every day for work, training and services, local centres are often denuded of people. However, often, older people are not looking for more social activities, but just regular contact with neighbours. Such contact can be facilitated by local shopping centres, villages with spatial "hearts", and places to stop and chat. Additionally, it was felt that more could be done to build cross-generational connections and support, with older people looking after the young, and young people helping to reduce isolation for the elderly.

High levels of disability associated with the retirement village in Kilmainhamwood, but also in Drumconrath

When comparisons of disability by age group are examined, the profile of the study area is skewed by the presence of the retirement village in Kilmainhamwood, where 60% of the population over 65 have a disability. This compares to 21% in Drumconrath, 42% in the study area generally, and 29% across County Meath. What is surprising though, is the high proportion of people with a disability in the 45 to 64 age group in Drumconrath at 44%, compared to 32% in the study area and 28% in the county.

Low proportion of professionals and high proportion of those never in paid employment

Social class information is available at ED level for the study area based on 2011 Census data. Taking the four EDs of the study area, 27% of its population were higher and lower professionals (social classes 1 and 2), which was lower than County Meath as a whole at 37%. The two villages had even less of their populations in the professional social classes at 22% and 17% in Drumconrath and Kilmainhamwood respectively. The study area as a whole had 20% of its population in the skilled manual class (social class 4), which was just slightly more than the county average at 18%. The two villages of Drumconrath and Kilmainhamwood both compared favourably at 16% and 18% respectively. However, the two villages hade high proportions of their populations who were unclassified (social class 7): 33% in Kilmainhamwood and 24% in Drumconrath, compared to 17% in the study area as a whole and 13% in County Meath. Social class 7 includes those who have never been in paid employment.

Local infrastructure, housing and the built environment

The case study area is not particularly well served by local infrastructure, such as public services and transport. However, given that it is a rural area with a small population (2 776), it could be argued that the area requires only a basic level of local infrastructure to meet needs, but more importantly, good access to services that are provided in the wider locality.

Large proportion of owner-occupied housing

In 2011, just over half of households in the study area owned their houses outright (51%), with a further 37% owner occupiers with a mortgage. Private renting was low at 4%, compared to 14% for the county as a whole. The housing tenure profile of the two villages was somewhat different, both containing a higher proportion of the population, (18%), renting from the local authority, compared to 5% in the study area and the county overall.

There is some public sector housing in the two villages of Drumconrath and Kilmainhamwood, with a limited number renting privately. The County Development Plan (Meath County Council, undated) states that 54 units are needed to meet the household target in Drumconrath, with 35 units required for Kilmainhamwood.

Local civic amenities complemented by those provided in neighbouring areas

There are a number of services provided locally. As outlined in the introduction, both villages have services such as primary schools, pre-schools, churches, shops, and sports grounds. Kilmainhamwood has a retirement village and hall, while Drumconrath has a number of other services, such as a community centre. Residents of this area also make use of services in nearby centres, such as in Nobber, Ardee and Kingscourt as well as further afield in Carrickmacross, Bailieborough, Kells, Dundalk and Navan. They travel to these towns for work, shopping, public services and social activities.

Poor accessibility and connections

Space syntax analysis reveals that both Kilmainhamwood Village and Drumconrath are not particularly accessible, but occur at intersections in the secondary rural road network with a lack of good connections into larger local towns and urban centres. Access to services is a particular issue for young people, old people, and others with limited mobility because of unemployment, disability or with caring responsibilities.

A further issue of accessibility is the peripheral location of housing developments in the villages in relation to the services provided in the village centres. In Drumconrath, in particular, the social housing estates are located on the outside of the village, so that it is a good walk to access the services of the village – shops, community centre, etc. This restricts accessibility for those with limited mobility. At the same time this undermines the ability of the villages' centres to form meeting points and to have sufficient footfall to support additional businesses and services. Given that elderly people often report feeling isolated, the existence of "village centres" would provide a good opportunity for socialising and the types of random encounter between neighbours which can be important in building relations of mutual support.

Challenges in maintaining extensive network of small roads

Transport and access to services is one of the key infrastructural requirements of living in a relatively remote, and somewhat disadvantaged, rural area. The level of car ownership was discussed earlier, but a key challenge for Meath County Council is maintenance of the extensive network of small roads in this area.

Public transport services available but with limitations

Public transport is also a key provision. There are four main service providers: the state bus service, Bus Eireann, which runs routes north-south through the area with connections to Kingscourt, Nobber and on to Navan and Dublin; a private bus company, Sillan Tours, which runs a daily commuter service from Cootehill in County Cavan, through Kingscourt, Nobber, Wilkinstown, Navan and Dunshaughlin en route to Dublin; a private bus company, Val Russell coaches (also known as Royal Breffni Tours and based in Kilmainhamwood) which runs a bus service through Kells and Bailieborough to Dundalk Institute of Technology; and Meath Accessible Transport who run a Flexibus community bus service.

However, it was felt by local stakeholders that a lack of accessible and affordable transport connections makes it difficult for people to undertake a number of activities important for their economic prosperity and wellbeing, including attending college, working at a distance from home and accessing services such as health and childcare.

Box 4.1. Priorities for future infrastructure development in the villages of Drumconrath and Kilmainhamwood

In terms of future infrastructural developments, Meath County Council has identified a number of challenges and objectives for the villages of Drumconrath and Kilmainhamwood. These include:

- Manage the sustainable development of the villages, appropriate to their size and scale.
- Protect and enhance the core of the villages, including conservation of any architectural features.
- Encourage the development of vacant, underused and derelict sites.
- Protect existing residential amenity and encourage the provision of additional housing to meet the changing demographics.
- Zone sufficient land to cater for local requirements for commercial, social, residential, community and recreational uses.

Source: Meath County Council (undated) "Meath County Development Plan 2013-2019, Volume 1", Written Statement.

Community Assets

North County Meath has a number of community assets. Notably, the people of north County Meath are an asset of the area, especially the strong sense of community. There are many family and local community networks of an informal nature. The large proportion of older people in the area is a potential asset in providing local activities and volunteers, although some capacity building may be required to realise this asset. People of working age have shown considerable flexibility in their approach to employment, and, of those who cannot find jobs within the area, many commute to jobs in other parts of the county, in neighbouring counties or as far as Dublin. There was also a notable entrepreneurial spirit among the young people.

Additionally, the area is relatively well served with local facilities such as sports facilities, schools, early education and childcare centres and a retirement village. Furthermore, the area contains a number of natural assets. As described earlier, the area is mainly comprised of agricultural land in an area of drumlins, particularly to the east. Thus, there are opportunities for the development of agricultural products and energy generation.

There is also the potential for tourism. There is a disused railway line from Navan to Kingscourt which runs through the area. There is a current proposal to develop this disused line as a Greenway. There would be a number of advantages for the local area, if such a Greenway were to be developed. It would draw tourists from Navan, the county's main town, up through the study area, and to Kilmainhamwood, in particular. There is potential to develop the old station at Kilmainhamwood, which could provide a coffee shop and/or outlet for local crafts and produce. It could also link with other walking and cycling routes in the adjacent area. Other options would be to maintain the tracks so that the railway line could be re-opened as a route back into Dublin in the future (reducing commuting times), or developed as a steam railway, which would also attract tourism. There are other tourism possibilities in the study area which could be developed, including water-based activities and angling in the local lakes, as well as the refurbishment of historic buildings for use as community, social or cultural centres.

Finally, the community spirit evident can also be seen in local enterprises. The most evident social enterprise operating in the area is the Flexibus service based in Navan. This has proved to be a valuable asset for a number of reasons: it provides a community transport service for the many older people living in the area; it provides employment; and it also provides job training and capacity building supports. There are also a number of other enterprises with social objectives, such as community childcare provision and credit unions in nearby towns.

The current policy response

To better understand how the issues identified above are currently being addressed, this section looks more closely at the overall local governance framework in Meath, as well as specific policy responses for social inclusion.

General local governance framework

Meath County Council is the primary unit of local government in the study area. The Council is mainly responsible for housing, local roads, planning and development, culture and leisure, community facilities, and waste collection throughout the county. The county has a system of area-based delivery through a network of one-stop shops, with a centre in Kells which covers the study area. There are 29 members on Meath Council, who are elected directly.

A number of changes in the County Council structure are taking place under the Local Government Reform Act 2014. Town Councils, such as Kells Town Council, have been abolished and are being replaced by Municipal Districts, which are based on population size. The study area falls under Kells Municipal District, which covers nearly a third (31.5%) of the county's area, and 15% of the county's population with a two thirds rural, one third urban spread. It also contains nearly a third of the county's roads.

Figure 4.5 provides an overview of the main policies and programmes delivered in the north County Meath study area to tackle poverty and disadvantage. It should be noted that, unlike in Blanchardstown, there are no programmes specifically targeted at the geographical area covered by the case study, but residents of the area can avail of programmes and services available in the locality. There are specific initiatives run at local level through local community groups and clubs.

There are a number of organisations whose remit is to provide services and support for the residents of the study area in north County Meath in relation to tackling poverty and disadvantage, however these are the main ones. It is worth noting, however, that the Department of Agriculture, Food and the Marine, and Teagasc (the farm advisory service), also have a role given the agricultural nature of much of the study area.

Figure 4.5. **Selected key institutional actors in north County Meath study area**

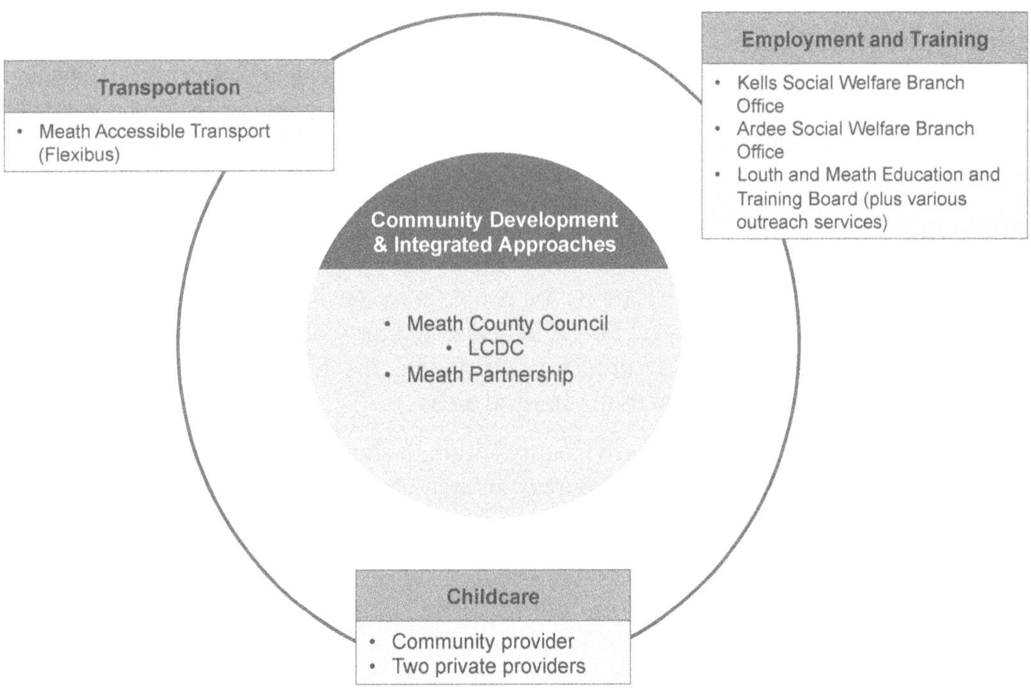

Area based approaches to community development

Before examining the institutional framework for specific issues, it is useful to look at the organisations that are taking an area-based approach to community development, predominantly Meath County Council (including the LCDC) and the Meath Partnership.

Meath County Council has a community and enterprise department which is concerned with social inclusion and community development throughout the county. The department has a focus on an integration strategy for Travellers and ethnic minorities, but as was outlined earlier, there are few ethnic minorities or Travellers in the study area. There is also an initiative promoting Meath as an "Age Friendly County" and this has implications for the retirement home in Kilmainhamwood. Much of the community activity is self-driven and there is an active community group in Drumconrath.

Meath County Council also has responsibility for the Local Community Development Committee which will oversee and co-ordinate the community development activities in the county, through a local economic and community plan. Meath will have an LCDC with a membership of 17, including elected members, Council staff, state agencies, representatives from Meath Partnership, the community and voluntary sector representatives, social inclusion interests, business and employers, environmental representatives, farming and agriculture interests, and the trade union sector. The Department of Housing, Planning, Community and Local Government-funded Social Inclusion and Community Activation Programme (SICAP), plus the new LEADER Programme (2014-2020) will be the first programmes to come within the oversight and management of the Committee. The economic element of the plan will be developed in parallel by the local authority.

Meath Partnership, based in Kells, is a county-wide community organisation responsible for the design and implementation of local, rural and community development programmes in Meath. The Partnership was established in 1996 as Meath LEADER, a rural development initiative, but has since emerged as Meath Partnership following a "cohesion process". The partnership has a specific focus on tackling disadvantage through a range of services and initiatives, including rural and community supports, as well as training and community employment.

In particular, Meath Partnership is responsible for delivering the Tús programme on behalf of the Department of Social Protection, where work experience is provided in community and voluntary organisations for people who are long-term unemployed. The Partnership also delivers the Rural Social Scheme, and provides rural supports, business training programmes and social initiatives, including the Men's Sheds project which provides a meeting place for men living in rural areas.

Finally, while not specific to north County Meath, it should be noted that there are also national policies/programmes that encourage an area-based approach specifically in rural areas, as described in Box 4.2.

Box 4.2. Other relevant national policies and programmes

In its 2013 report, the Commission for the Economic Development of Rural Areas (CEDRA) set out a range of recommendations for the development of Ireland's rural areas, many of which resonate with the economic and social needs of north County Meath. Especially relevant are the recommendations on the need for a policy co-ordination and delivery mechanism, the establishment of a Rural Innovation and Development Fund, and supports to facilitate economic and community participation, such as provision of broadband, access to finance and mobilising community capacity. Of interest is the recommendation for the piloting of Rural Economic Development Zones (REDZs), through the development and implementation of local strategic economic development plans. Although the study area in north County Meath is small, it could be encompassed within such a zone.

The new Rural Development Programme, due to run from 2014 to 2020, will also be relevant for north County Meath. It is envisaged that some elements of this programme will be applicable to the rural population in north County Meath, especially the LEADER element (Department of Agriculture, Food and the Marine, 2014). This will include rural tourism, enterprise development, broadband training, and building community capacity, as well as bottom-up approaches to local development and supports for distinctive regional products and artisan food producers.

Specific policy areas

Income support, employment, education and training

For income support and employment services people in the west of the study area around Kilmainhamwood are likely to go to Kells social welfare branch office, while those in the east of the study area around Drumconrath are likely to go to Ardee in County Louth. The operation of the Kells office is franchised to a self-employed contractor, who employs staff to deliver the service. The information to process claims is collected at local branch level but sent to the main office in Navan for decisions, as this is where the staff of the Department of Social Protection are located. The decisions are sent back to the Kells local branch for further processing and payment. An Intreo office, which will provide the suite of employment and income support services in a "one-stop shop", is being established in Navan. However, the branch offices in Kells and Ardee will be retained. People will be assessed and paid in the branch offices, although the decisions are made in Navan.

There is group engagement and one-to-one support provided in Kells and Ardee. Regarding recipients of social welfare payments, people in receipt of working age payments in the Kells office are asked to participate in group engagement and a one-to-one interview with a case officer as part of the activation process. Given the rural nature of the study area, some people from the area may be engaged on the Rural Social Scheme (RSS) run by the Meath Partnership. The RSS is aimed at low-income farmers (and fishermen/women) who are receiving a social welfare payment. Participants on the RSS provide services that are of benefit to rural communities, for example, maintaining walking routes, social care of older people, energy conservation and village enhancement projects. There are also some opportunities for people through the Gateway programme where long-term unemployed people can get work experience with Meath County Council, and through the Tús programme. However, because of the limited number of employers in the area, and the fact that many are small employers, there are restricted opportunities for programmes like JobBridge and JobsPlus.

Louth Meath Education and Training Board, based in Navan, is responsible for providing vocational education and training to the people from the study area. Louth Meath Education and Training Board is a merger of County Meath Vocational Education Committee (VEC) and Louth VEC. The merger took place on 1 July 2013 and some of the arrangements are still being put in place.

A range of education courses is provided through the ETB. There is a Youthreach Centre (for early school leavers) in Kells, and also an Adult Guidance Service there. Adult education fee-paying courses are provided in Nobber. O'Carolan College, which is a comprehensive secondary school with DEIS status, is located in Nobber.[7] Vocational education and training courses are also provided in Kingscourt in Cavan. Community education opportunities are available for community groups in the north Meath area and they can apply for grants for tutors. Vocational Training Opportunities Scheme (VTOS) services are only available in Navan, and there is no "FAS" training centre in Meath, with the closest one being in Dundalk, County Louth. Dundalk also has the closest third-level college at the Institute of Technology. However, it was felt by local stakeholders that access to education and training facilities was not optimal due to the lack of affordable transport connections, which had a knock on impact on people's motivation to learn.

Because relatively few courses are provided in the study area, people who want to do courses have to travel to other centres, such as Nobber, Kells, Navan, Kingscourt, or Dundalk. Accessibility is, therefore, a significant issue. People either have to have access to a car or a lift or rely on one of the bus services. The suitability of these transport options may depend on the time and venue of the course. Cost is also a factor for some people in attending education and training courses. While some courses are free, others have to be paid for. In addition, car parking costs in some of the urban centres where courses are provided are high, e.g. in Kells and Navan. There is an "E-Learning" mobile van which can be taken to the area, but the limited broadband coverage restricts its use in north County Meath.

In addition, as a result of the economic recession and institutional reform, the resources of the ETB have been reduced so that it can be difficult, in some instances, to meet demand. For example, while the proposed conversion of the disused railway line may bring jobs to the area, it was noted that there is a skills gap in the tourism and hospitality sector. Further efforts may be needed to retrain people from their existing skills sets into new employment areas. To do this, a skills audit may be required to understand the types of skills that people currently have, and the degree to which there is a possibility to transition into new areas of work.

Career guidance for both young people and adults appears to need investment. It was acknowledged that there had been cut-backs in career guidance and that its restoration and/or development would help provide young people, in particular, with a range of options for their future careers. A key focus for career guidance would be the progression of people from training and education into work. Such progression is an objective of both providers and receivers of education and training services, yet this can be difficult in the study area where there are limited options and jobs available for people.

Finally, the Local Enterprise Office (LEO) in Navan, County Meath is now the front-line state service for those wishing to start or expand a business. In addition to providing a range of financial and non-financial supports to assist enterprises at the start-up and expansion phases, the LEO provides training, mentoring and a signposting service to other state services for micro and small enterprises. However, overall, it is felt that more could be done to boost the aspirations of start-up companies, and to provide motivational support and skills development for those wishing to set up a new business.

Transportation

Physical access is a significant issue for the population of the study area in north County Meath, in relation to both transport links and telecommunications access. Many people are dependent on cars for transport to jobs and services, and car ownership is relatively high, probably out of necessity (although as noted earlier it is more limited in the villages of Drumconrath and Kilmainhamwood). There is an issue of road maintenance in the study area with an intricate network of small roads covering a wide area. The road network is difficult for Meath County Council to maintain and it hinders accessibility for people living in the area due to the poor quality of the roads. The poor condition of the roads also adds to the cost of car maintenance. As discussed earlier, there are public, private and community bus services in the area, but these all have limitations in terms of accessibility of bus stops, routes and timetables.

Meath Accessible Transport Project, running Flexibus, is the community transport group operating in the Meath area, as part of the government's Rural Transport Programme, which was set up to address the shortfall in available public transport in rural areas, see Box 4.3. There have been structural changes made to the Rural Transport Programme at the national level. The 35 Rural Transport Groups that were delivering services were amalgamated into 18 National Transport Co-ordination Units, with a group operating in every rural county. Additionally, the management of the Rural Transport Scheme has been transferred from Pobal to the National Transport Authority. There is now greater pressure to run the service commercially.

As the name suggests, the National Transport Co-ordination Units, which will be linked to local authorities, will devise and co-ordinate a public transport plan for their area. The Meath Accessible Transport Project Ltd., which runs Flexibus, will be part of the Meath/Louth/Fingal Transport Co-ordination Unit, which will also include North Fingal Rural Transport Company Ltd. and Louth Leadership Partnership Ltd.

Box 4.3. **Flexibus**

Meath Accessible Transport, running Flexibus, was set up in 1999. It provides rural transport for the whole of County Meath, along with some services to adjoining counties, such as to Bailieborough and Kingscourt in County Cavan.

Flexibus provides transport services to the people living in Drumconrath and Kilmainhamwood and their environs, taking people to Carrickmacross, Bailiborough and Navan for shopping and other services, and to Nobber for bingo. Flexibus provides a door-to-door service with prospective passengers making an appointment in advance. Users of the service are predominantly older women who have a free travel pass. Flexibus also provides a community car scheme.

Meath Accessible Transport owns a fleet of 19 buses (from 8 seaters up to 18 seaters), unlike some other community transport providers who do not own buses but contract other transport operators to provide a community service. As a community enterprise, Meath Accessible Transport utilises schemes such as Tús and community employment in providing the service. All drivers receive training and many current drivers who came through this route are now providing training to others.

Family and children's services

There are three childcare providers in the study area, one community (in Kilmainhamwood) and two private (both in Drumconrath). There are also opportunities for community groups to apply for grants for tutors for community education. Where childcare may be a potential barrier to participation in education and training courses there is a scheme for people on authorised educational courses to get reduced childcare costs (where the childcare providers are registered for this initiative).

A local co-ordinating mechanism is the County Children and Young People's Services Committee. An audit of services and needs analysis of children's services in County Meath, carried out by the Meath Children and Young People's Services Committee (Quigley et al., 2013), found that the county as a whole is one of the most poorly funded counties in terms of youth provision, despite having a disproportionately high number of young people living in the county. While the study area in north County Meath is under-represented in terms of young people, there are very few services for young people and teenagers in the area. Young people have to travel to Nobber, Kells or Navan to access services, or go to towns in the neighbouring counties of Cavan, Monaghan and Louth. An ongoing challenge for the Meath Children and Young People's Services Committee is to ensure that children and young people in all parts of the county, including the study area in the north, have access to appropriate services and facilities. This problem is compounded by a lack of staffing for initiatives, such as summer schools, in the area. A further issue here is the lack of DEIS primary schools in the area, which means that problems of educational disadvantage are not being addressed early enough in the life-cycle.

Cross-cutting challenges

Concerns about the implementation of some national policies, especially in a rural context

A recurring theme in Meath was that policy decisions made nationally and internationally often have unintended negative impacts locally. Examples include the way in which national tendering schemes are organised and the way in which EU agricultural quotas are allocated. Like in Blanchardstown, the lack of local flexibility was continually raised as an issue. There have been many institutional changes in relation to the delivery of social welfare, employment support programmes, education and training initiatives and community supports which have implications for the delivery of services at local level. Many of these services are driven from the "top-down" and it was suggested that greater consideration needs to be given to what is required at the local level, or a "bottom-up" view.

Additionally, there was a sentiment expressed that often national policies were designed with urban areas in mind, without adequate consideration given to their implementation in rural areas. In terms of funding, issues related to short-term funding cycles, as well as parity in funding across areas. As a result, as was raised in one roundtable, some people in the community are hesitant to avail themselves of public services because of a fear that these services will subsequently be cut.

Further, when measuring the impact of programmes, it was felt that there was too much emphasis on numbers and throughput as measures of success. In rural areas, the numbers may be small but specific interventions may have a significant and lasting impact – these qualitative impacts also need to be measured.

Recent reforms have promise, but implementation remains a challenge

Much attention is being given to the role of the recently established Local Community Development Committees (LCDCs) in providing a framework for the development of disadvantaged areas. This may provide a challenge for the Meath LCDC, however, as the study area comprises only 1.5% of the population of the county, and the Committee's attention may be drawn elsewhere. A key concern of people in the study area is how the LCDC will connect to the needs of the communities in north County Meath. An important dimension of the LCDC will be the involvement of employers, with a view to better linking people and jobs.

Issues of local capacities to successfully deliver on recent reforms were also raised. Not only were overall staffing levels raised as an issue during the study tour, but it was also noted that in order for the LCDC to play its role as a community convener, it will need the requisite leadership and capacity behind it. It was seen to be important that local people come up with ideas and lead on their implementation, rather than relying on external people to do things for them. Additionally, in the context of the Intreo reforms, it was noted that working with employers will be a new task for many DSP staff, and skills in this area will have to be built.

Finally, the lines of communication between national and local actors were raised as an issue. For example, it was noted that information about national policy changes (such as the development of the LCDCs, the new opportunities around LEADER and SICAP) could be communicated better to local actors, so that misunderstandings are minimised and a common understanding is built of government priorities and the potential for local development. Communication needs to be clearer and without jargon.

More co-ordinated approach needed

As in the Blanchardstown area, the role of local and informal networks in co-ordinating services at the local level was highlighted. The limited extent to which local networks can broker solutions between agencies was acknowledged, and this may reflect the degree of flexibility local managers have within national agencies and policy frameworks, as discussed earlier. It was felt that when joining up and co-ordination did occur this was mainly personality-driven and therefore not sustainable. Staffing embargoes meant that people did not have the time required to work on co-ordination and facilitation. There was a lack of understanding of all the different services available, meaning that a mapping of different interventions would be useful (this has been done for under 18s but for not older age groups). It was felt that there was the potential for local organisations to collaborate further on funding applications and develop combined approaches, therefore maximising impacts on the ground. However, it was noted that often, local areas report data to the national level, but then subsequently, this data is never fed back down to the local level. This impedes the ability of local actors to use this data to develop shared strategies, co-ordinate their work and support ongoing programme improvement.

Potential for social enterprises

Social enterprises could potentially contribute further to tackling problems of poverty and social inclusion in Meath. They could, in particular, help in addressing a number of issues that are very common in rural areas such as physical and social isolation, the decline of rural services resulting from an increase in commuting, and an ageing population. Internationally, there is a wide range of experiences to draw on within the social economy sector, including: agri-tourism; farmers markets; the development of ecological/organic products; and other forms of food processing. One example is the Association Mozaik in Slovenia, which has built on local cultural and natural assets to foster social inclusion for disadvantaged people, while enhancing the quality of life of the local community. Another project, O4O, has focused on the co-production of services with older people (see Box 4.4).

Overlapping administrative boundaries cause particular challenges

As highlighted earlier, the study area, while located in north County Meath, borders the counties of Cavan, Monaghan and Louth, with many residents of the study area travelling to these counties for work, to access services and for social and recreational activities. In addition, many service providers, for example the Department of Social Protection, use different boundaries in relation to the administration of social welfare payments, so that those in the east of the study area go to Ardee in County Louth, while those in the west go to Kells, located in County Meath. As a result, DSP representatives from the same office are involved in several different LCDCs, stretching their resources and capacities.

The lack of alignment of boundaries across the various agencies can make it challenging to ensure that the needs of people living in the study area are met, and that there is not duplication. To adequately meet the needs of people living in the area requires agencies and organisations to work closely together, and the evidence suggests that this does not always happen, especially where there is competition for scarce resources.

Box 4.4. Social enterprise in rural communities

O4O: Older people for older people

"Older people for older people" has worked with rural communities in Scotland, Greenland, Sweden and Northern Ireland to identify older people's need for basic services and to enhance their health and wellbeing. The project has engendered life-long learning in older people and helped them to flourish as assets within their local communities. The focus was on helping older people to identify their own needs, while supporting them to develop a variety of social organisations to meet these needs. In part, the aim was that older people could live happily and healthily in their own homes and communities for longer. Learning from the project was used to shape a future agenda for older people's service provision through social enterprise. Practical recommendations were also developed on the need for changes to local, national and international policies in order to develop "community co-production" of services (see http://www.o4os.eu/policy-briefings.asp).

The key message from this project is that although the process of generating positive impact can be lengthy, difficult and fragile, this can produce worthwhile benefits. It was found that policy and service delivery motivations must be transparent to motivate people to buy in. The project also showed that new structures are needed to make social enterprises work as service providers for rural areas: it was found that "Integrated service hubs may be suitable for small communities, but they, too, would need structure, force and leadership to function successfully. Structures such as enabling public sector employees to volunteer for one day a year could contribute to wide-scale changes".

Source: Munoz, S.A. Dr., Prof. J. Farmer, K. Stephen et al. (n.d.), "Achieving Social Enterprise Development in Rural Communities", *O4O Policy Briefing No. 2.*, www.o4os.eu/userfiles/file/_General_Documents/Policy%20Briefing%202.pdf.

Association Mozaik

Association Mozaik in Slovenia (http://www.inovum.si/social/en/news/20) was established in 2003, with the aim of addressing social inclusion for the most disadvantaged, and improving the quality of life of the local community. It does this by linking local cultural traditions in the deprived region of Pomurje, to productive activities (traditional building, eco-agriculture and food production, and environmental services), and to employment and training activities. In addition, it aims to develop a distinctive mentoring expertise for assisting disadvantaged people. The association's training and work integration programmes emphasise practical work, and it draws in outside experts to assist with training – so far more than 200 disadvantaged people have been assisted.

Mozaik develops permanent employment through activities such as: ecological agriculture and food processing; traditional building using natural materials (straw, wood, clay, flax and linen, straw and birch); environmental services in regional parks (maintenance of cycling paths, hiking paths, waterways); and agricultural land management. One of the key strategies for achieving this is through eco-social farms – providing permanent employment opportunities for disadvantaged groups. An eco-social farm in Šalovci (Goričko area) was established in 2008. Initially, it was renovated to maintain its traditional characteristics and then an Employment Centre (sheltered workshop) was established providing regular employment for 11 people with disabilities, as well as training facilities for many others.

Their approach to marketing involves developing their own brand, and opening a variety of marketing channels for: direct sales, on farm sales, the tourist market, and for public procurement, such as for schools and public bodies. Financially, the association has been successful in gaining EU programme finance, as well as grants from various Slovenian Ministries. So far it has around 20% of its income from the market (including sales of its own produce).

Source: Spear, R. et al. (2010), "Improving Social Inclusion at the Local Level Through the Social Economy: Report for Slovenia", http://dx.doi.org/10.1787/5kg0nvfx2g26-en

Poor road and broadband infrastructure have knock-on effects

A recurring theme was the knock-on effects that poor road and broadband infrastructure have in the area. In particular, broadband access can be considered a "lynchpin" for everything from entrepreneurship to accessing services to training and education. In 2012, the government announced a new broadband initiative, *Delivering A Connected Society.* This National Broadband Plan sets out a strategy to deliver high speed broadband throughout Ireland. A High Level Implementation Group, chaired by the Department of Communications, Energy and Natural Resources, has been established to oversee the implementation of the plan. More specifically, in April 2014 the Minister for Communications, Energy and Natural Resources announced a proposed intervention to deliver high quality and reliable high speed broadband, including major fibre build-out, to rural areas. A mapping process will assess where the commercial sector will provide high speed broadband over the coming years. This will also identify those areas where a state intervention will be necessary.

Conclusion

North County Meath is not alone in the challenges it is facing; rural regions across the OECD are facings similar obstacles. Many of the components of the OECD's New Rural Paradigm (see Table 4.2), developed in 2006 to help guide member countries in taking a more nuanced approach to rural development, are relevant for the case study area.

Table 4.2. **The New Rural Paradigm**

	Old approach	New approach
Objectives	Equalisation, farm income, farm competitiveness	Competitiveness of rural areas, developing local assets, exploitation of unused resources
Key target sector	Agriculture	Various sectors of rural economies (e.g. rural tourism, manufacturing, ICT, industries, etc.)
Main tools	Subsidies	Investments
Key actors	National governments, farmers	All levels of government (supra-national, national, regional and local), various local stakeholders (public, private, non-governmental)

Source: OECD (2006), *The New Rural Paradigm: Policies and Governance.*

Ensuring that the residents of north County Meath are able to contribute to and benefit from more inclusive growth will require a multi-pronged approach, with efforts needed both on the development side and the services side across governance levels. The importance of a multi-level governance approach is one of the characteristics of the "new rural paradigm" described above. For example, addressing the area's poor broadband infrastructure is a key priority that the county cannot tackle on its own. The roll-out of the government's new broadband strategy represents an important step forward in addressing this problem. Additionally, better co-ordination of policies and services is needed, both between national and local actors as well as between local actors working on the ground.

There are also some actions local actors can take more directly. The development of local assets is another component of the "new rural paradigm", and in Meath there are a large number of community assets that could be better leveraged in the case study area. For example, local facilities, such as schools, have the potential to be used by the community for training, broadband access, etc. in the evenings and on weekends. Consideration could also be given to how to use the land in new ways, such as alternative energy production. The strong sense of community and entrepreneurial spirit could feed into the development of alternative economic models, such as co-operatively owned pubs and stores or the expansion of the social enterprise sector.

Notes

1. Most of the data available for this section is drawn from the 2011 Census of Population, which is the most recent source of data available at this level of disaggregation.
2. The age dependency rate is the population aged 0-14 plus the population aged 65 and over as a percentage of the population aged 15 to 64.
3. These figures are from Census 2011. As noted earlier, these are the most recent statistics available at this level of disaggregation.
4. "Other service activities" comprise activities of membership organisations, repair of computers and personal and household goods, washing and dry-cleaning, hairdressing and other beauty treatment, funeral and related activities, physical wellbeing activities, and other activities not economically classified.
5. This was articulated at the roundtable discussions, but specific data is not available on this topic. However, in the nearby town of Kells (where there are more employment opportunities than in the study area; with 1 386 jobs being recorded in the 2011 Census), there are 2 111 people living in the Kells area who are classed as being "at work". Of these, 22% (464) are employed in Kells, 38% (806) are employed elsewhere in Meath, and 25% (537) commute out of the county for employment. The remaining 14% (304) are either mobile workers or have an uncodeable destination. There is a daily net loss of working population in the Kells area of -421 (van Egeraat & Gleeson, 2013: 39).
6. The information is presented at "small area level" for the four Electoral Divisions of the study area. Each "small area" contains an average of 90 households.
7. DEIS is Delivering Equality of Opportunity in Schools. It is essentially a designation as a school serving a disadvantaged area or pupils and as such gets access to additional resources.

Chapter 5

Conclusions and recommendations for improving social inclusion in Ireland

This chapter presents the conclusions and recommendations related to improving social inclusion in Ireland, drawing particularly on the findings from two case studies areas. In particular, it looks at issues related to improving governance and building capacities; better leveraging community assets; and increasing accessibility to economic opportunity. It concludes with a number of priorities for action at the national and local levels.

This chapter looks across the national socio-economic context in Ireland, the review of the measures currently in place to address disadvantage and promote inclusive growth, and the two case studies to identify the following conclusions and area recommendations. Following the main themes of the project, the conclusions and recommendations fall into three key categories: 1) improving governance and building capacities; 2) leveraging existing assets; and 3) improving accessibility to economic opportunity. The chapter concludes by identifying a number of recommendations for immediate action at the national and local levels.

Improving governance and building capacities

Co-ordination at the local level remains a key gap

The recent governance reforms offer promise in terms of improving the ability of local actors to collaborate to tackle disadvantage, for example through the LCDCs and the establishment of Intreo. As noted earlier, the new Intreo service provides a seminal step change in the integration of services for the unemployed, as it brings together income support and employment services in the one organisational entity at local level, with outreach to employers. Furthermore, linkages are being developed with local education and training providers, as the basis for further integration.

However, outstanding issues around governance and capacities remain. Further work may be required in rationalising the service offerings of these agencies to ensure there are more streamlined pathways to assist people back into employment. Another issue was the need to improve co-ordination between various actors working at the local level. For example, Blanchardstown is currently a very "crowded platform", with many different actors pursuing different activities. This has the benefit of creating overlapping social capital networks, but it also risks a relatively high degree of fragmentation.

One approach seen in other OECD countries, to better co-ordinate work horizontally, is the use of local brokers who act as intermediaries between organisations across a broad set of policy areas. These brokers could play a key role in mapping local service provision, for example, by working with local service users to identify the main gaps and overlaps. This could include secondees from elsewhere in the public and private/not-for-profit sector, although there is also merit in building capacities by appointing somebody local. The advantage of a brokerage role is that it does not require a significant amount of resources, but it can make a difference across many different policy areas. Box 5.1 provides two examples of how this has been approached in other OECD countries. For co-ordinating services for particular individuals, key workers can play a parallel role, but at the level of individuals as opposed to organisations. Such positions would complement the joint strategic planning, which will occur with the LCDCs, by encouraging more joined-up working on the ground.

At the county level, it will be important that the county governments and the LCDCs bring the activities of the LEOs and local and community development programmes into coherent social and economic strategies, which also include a consideration of geography, accessibility and space. As the LCDCs themselves have limited resources, they will succeed or fail to the extent that they leverage other programmes and funds to common goals, and draw in the skills of other local actors. However, there are some concerns that a lack of flexibility in national initiatives and programmes will mean that it will be difficult to adjust and tailor them as part of broader local strategies.

Box 5.1. The role of brokers in Canada and Australia

Business and industry liaison officers (BILS) in Alberta, Canada

In Alberta, Canada, specific job roles have been developed and intermediaries employed to enable labour market officials to engage horizontally with a broad set of policy areas to solve problems. These include the Business and Industry Liaison Officers (BILS). These brokers catalyse cross-sector policy responses, provide linkages to employers, and contribute to resolving short-term collective problems. The BILS help the Government of Alberta (Alberta Employment and Immigration) to reach out to industry and employers, e.g. by holding workshops on employee attraction and retention, and diversity awareness. In the town of Wetaskiwin, for example, it was identified how this officer had played a catalyst role in setting up a daycare service, and facilitated the provision of new transport for rural communities – evidence of officers' ability to facilitate cross-sector policy responses to urgent local problems. In order to secure industry information and consultation, the Department of Post-Secondary Education, Training and Labour also funds the salaries of the Labour Force Development Officer positions in the Enterprise Agencies under a defined contractual agreement.

Source: Froy, F. et al. (2011), "Building Flexibility and Accountability Into Local Employment Services: Synthesis of OECD Studies in Belgium, Canada, Denmark and the Netherlands", OECD Local Economic and Employment Development (LEED) Working Papers, 2011/10, OECD Publishing. http://dx.doi.org/10.1787/5kg3mkv3tr21-en

Local Employment Co-ordinators in vulnerable areas, Australia

Australia's Keep Australia Working strategy made the co-ordination of employment policies at the local level a priority. In each Priority Employment Area, Local Employment Co-ordinators (LECs) were appointed to assist in driving local responses to local labour market problems. The Local Employment Co-ordinator was an agent of the federal government and their main role was to:

- Identify the needs of the area and match people with employment, education and training opportunities
- Target business and industries to identify emerging employment opportunities
- Develop and maintain a relationship with local Advisory Committees
- Identify skills and labour shortages, and structural barriers that compromise job matching
- Identify projects or activities which may be funded through allocated federal funding – a Flexible Funding Pool – and which will deliver employment and skills development outcomes.

However, this role was discontinued in 2014/2015.

Source: OECD (2014c), *OECD Reviews on Local Job Creation – Australia.*

To this end, attention should also be paid to whether it makes sense to create co-ordinating mechanisms above and below the county level to complement the LCDCs. At the supra-county level, in Blanchardstown, there is a need to take account of its role both as a residential location and as a site of large employers within the Greater Dublin functional urban area. Many of the problems of Blanchardstown's growth in the past two decades (such as a concentration of social housing, a mismatch between the skills sought by local employers and the skills profile of local residents, and a concentration of immigrants with language barriers) can only be addressed by a coherent approach at city-regional level. This applies to decisions on inward investment, improving access to the labour market, support for immigrant integration, and social housing provision. Because the Meath study area borders three counties and DSP boundaries cut across these areas, attention needs to be paid to cross-county co-ordination.

Below the county level, there is a need to ensure that the County Councils, the LCDCs, and other stakeholders are able to address disadvantage at the very local level. For example, in Meath the study area's population is less than 2% of the total population of the county. Smaller, more homogenous areas, such as Blanchardstown, may benefit from a more joined up approach to very local problems, such as drugs issues. In the past, the RAPID designation played this role, but this initiative has largely been disbanded. While more general reforms to employment policy, training and local government in mainstream services will surely have broad reaching effects, they may not be sufficient on their own to catalyse broader changes in communities where multiple disadvantages are particularly concentrated. Within the LCDCs, there is scope – and even an obligation – to develop the sub-structures necessary to tackle area-specific and issue-specific matters, and there are examples of LCDCs outside of the case study areas that have done so. In County Kildare, for example, a range of sub-structures have been developed below LCDC level to secure the flexibility and focus required to address area-related matters – these sub-structures have been established to cover three towns (Kildare, Kilcock and Celbridge) and ensure a focus on the issues of importance in those areas. Dublin City Council is also in the process of establishing area related sub-structures to secure a similar flexibility and focus.

In the short-term, this type of focus on integrating services and better co-ordination in "pockets" of disadvantage may have more traction and be more scalable than an approach that provides additional financial resources. Securing high-level buy-in for such an approach would be critical. At the national level, it will require that flexibility be injected into policy frameworks, so that local stakeholders are able to adjust policies and programmes as needed. At the local level, buy-in will also be needed, given funding could not be used as a "carrot" to induce change. However, it is important to acknowledge that, while an integrated services approach has the benefits of being more "scalable", in the long-term, additional resources and capacities may be needed for local areas such as Blanchardstown which are facing challenges that are actually national in scope, but local in manifestation. Creative approaches to ring-fencing public and private resources, such as through procurement processes, could be a complement to these efforts.

Following a series of public sector reforms, limited local capacities pose a challenge

As the local authorities take on their new, expanded role, there is a strong need for capacity building – particularly given that this is the first time that many of them will have this level of responsibility for issues such as social inclusion. There are technical skills and expertise to be built. At the same time, OECD LEED has identified some key areas where additional generic skills are required to build effective co-operation at the local level, including creativity and problem solving skills, analytical skills, strategic skills, leadership skills, and partnership skills (Froy and Giguère, 2010). In Ontario, Canada, a Change Management Office was set up to oversee the transfer of staff from the federal to provincial government and it helped to bridge different organisational cultures and work processes. Similar organisation could be considered for Ireland to ensure a smooth transition phase (see Box 5.2 for other approaches to building local capacities).

Box 5.2. Approaches to building local level capacities

Community Capacity Building in Newfoundland and Labrador

The Department of Innovation, Business and Rural Development in Newfoundland and Labrador, Canada offers a community capacity building programme to economic development organisations in order to build their capacity to be partners in regional economic development. The programme provides non-repayable contributions to not-for-profit economic development organisations such as municipalities, industry/sector groups, educational institutions and any other community based organisation involved in economic development. In addition, it provides training and supports development sessions based on a series of certified programme modules. These modules include sessions on the following topics: strategic planning; relationship building; organisational skills and management; and co-operative development.

Strong Cities, Strong Communities

In order to help the American cities hardest hit by the recession, the Strong Cities, Strong Communities (SC2) initiative is a new model of federal-local collaboration, intended to improve how the federal government works with local governments to further job creation and local economic development. It includes several strands. Inter-agency federal SC2 teams work with selected cities to help them better navigate existing federal agencies and programmes, while providing technical assistance and expertise. Additionally, through the SC2 fellowship programme, early- to mid-career professionals complete two-year fellowships in mayor's offices or local government agencies to assist in the design and implementation of strategic projects. Another strand is the economic visioning challenge, through which federal supports are provided to cities to help them implement a "challenge competition" in which teams of professionals submit economic development proposals, with the best proposal receiving a financial prize. Finally, through the SC2 National Resource Network, several types of technical assistance are available, including direct support, access to peer networks, and on-line tools and resources.

Source: Skinner, G. (2012), "Department of Innovation, Business and Rural Development, Government of Newfoundland and Labrador", http://www.oecd.org/rural/krasnoyarsk/3%20Gillian%20Skinner_MR2_Skill%20Building_ENG.pdf; White House Council (2013), "Strong Cities, Strong Communities Initiative", *1st Annual Report, April 2013*, http://www.huduser.org/portal/publications/pdf/huddoc.pdf

It appears that rural areas are particularly suffering from a lack of capacity. It will be important to recognise and re-affirm the value of community development in rural areas, utilising the planned new European Community Led Local Development (CLLD approach) for 2014-2020 as a global grant for inclusive rural development, with a small grants programme for local social capital (as set out in the recent Report of the Commission for the Economic Development of Rural Areas (CEDRA)). Fingal County could also consider lobbying for the use of the new Community Led Local Development provisions in the Operational Programmes for ESF and ERDF. The Fingal LCDC could then become the responsible body for community-led local development in the area, which would bring resources and a clear methodology within which to operate. It will also be important to consider opportunities within the new European LEADER programme for 2015-2020 – local projects can apply for funding on the basis that they are aligned with a local objective in the local development strategy and also correspond with the specific LEADER themes (Social Inclusion, Economic Development/Job Creation, Rural Environment) and sub-themes (Rural Tourism, Enterprise Development, Rural Towns, Broadband, Provision of services targeted at hard to reach communities, Rural Youth etc.).

National policies can have unintended local consequences

National policies and public service personnel need to have sufficient flexibility at local level, within national frameworks, to deliver programmes tailored to local circumstances and people's needs. There is a need for more locally sensitive mainstream employment services to address local bottlenecks around getting people into jobs, for example, through childcare provision, or the availability of ESOL courses.

In a broader sense, there seems to be a need to improve policy coherence and communication at the national level. In the context of the wide range of reforms described in Chapter 2, local actors need a consistent and well-organised approach to current changes so as to fully invest in the new system. Evidence collected during the study tour suggests that this remains a gap.

More consideration is also needed for how national and regional policies impact local areas in various ways, both positive and negatively. But, the onus is not just on national and regional actors: ad hoc local implementation of national policies can impede their intended impact.

For example, land use, planning and housing allocation policy has resulted in compounding many of the issues of disadvantage which are evident in the Blanchardstown area. Currently, Memoranda to Government require a statement on impact, specifically in relation to a proposal's impact on poverty, rural communities, employment, and gender (as well as cost to the Exchequer, north-south, east-west relations, industry costs and quality regulation). A framework has been developed to assist in carrying out poverty impact assessment.[1] Additionally, the establishment of the regional assemblies in January 2015 aims to help better co-ordinate national, regional and local policies, an approach that will be strengthened by the National Planning Framework and Regional Spatial and Economic Strategies (late 2016-early 2017).

Both the National Spatial Strategy (and any successor) and the Regional Spatial and Economic Strategies (to be adopted by Ireland's regional assemblies) should consider further how to move away from planning policies which lead to concentrations of people in need in low density peripheral areas, while ensuring the provision of more compact and dense affordable housing in the centre of cities and towns. As pointed out by the OECD (2014a), the Regional Spatial and Economic Strategies could be a particularly effective co-ordination mechanism as they better reflect functional economic areas rather than administrative boundaries.

In developing new social housing, more consideration needs to be given to accessibility to local services, amenities and economic opportunities, and integration into the broader urban fabric at both the local and regional scales. For example, it is important to ensure that when social housing is built in rural areas it is well connected into the centre of rural villages and to local amenities, to ensure more pedestrian through movement in the estates, to support pedestrian use of services, and to preserve local amenities and spaces in which (sometimes isolated) people can gather. Finally, the push for increased "tendering out" of employment support and other community programmes should be kept under review. While there are efficiency gains that can be realised from such tendering, these gains are not a foregone conclusion. In particular, attention needs to be paid to ensuring tendering is not creating undue competition (as opposed to collaboration) at the local level, and is actually meeting the needs of the local communities, not leaving gaps in provision, as well as providing best value for money in the longer term.

A more data-driven and evidence-based approach is needed

Efforts to promote inclusive growth and tackle disadvantage could also benefit from a more data-driven and evidence-based approach. For example, there is a need for more rigorous evaluation on "what works" in getting disconnected people back to work, including better understanding of best practice within the not-for-profit sector, the local development companies, and national schemes such as Tús, Momentum, and Gateway. As outlined in the Box 5.3, several OECD countries have recently established "what works centres" to better collect and collate evaluation evidence.

At the front end, there is also room to build a stronger "data infrastructure". This includes developing common definitions of key types of data (for example, what constitutes an output, indicator, and cost) as well as using agreed administrative boundaries so that the impact of policies, programmes and services in specific places can be adequately monitored.

Box 5.3. "What Works Centres"

A number of countries, including Denmark, Sweden, the United States and the United Kingdom have established national "knowledge" or "what works" centres in recent years for the purpose of improving the dissemination and use of evaluation evidence. Two of these are described in more detail below.

Denmark

The Danish Agency for Labour Market and Recruitment launched a new evidence strategy in response to increasing interest from politicians about the effects of active labour market policies. This strategy is based on three pillars:

- **Collect existing evidence.** Researchers are funded to conduct literature reviews of existing impact studies, including drawing conclusions about overall effects. Each of the studies is catalogued in a "knowledge bank".
- **Develop new evidence.** The agency is implementing pilot projects, in which the overall framework is defined nationally, but municipalities have the flexibility to specify the details of programme design and implementation. In this way, it is able to learn about the relationship between different programme designs and impacts. Additionally, it is also funding randomised controlled trials of programmes, considered the "gold standard" of measuring impacts.
- **Communicate/disseminate the results.** Finally, to communicate/disseminate results, the agency holds conferences, sends out a monthly newsletter, and has developed an online "knowledge bank", where existing studies can be easily searched and accessed.

United Kingdom

In 2013, the United Kingdom launched a "What Works" Initiative based on the principle that good decision-making should be informed by the best available evidence on both what works and what does not work. The "What Works" network is composed of seven independent What Works Centres in the following policy areas: health and social care, educational achievement, crime reduction, early intervention, local economic growth, improved quality of life for older people, and wellbeing. The centres are funded through a combination of government and non-government sources, including the Economic and Social Research Council and the Big Lottery Fund.

The What Works Centre for Local Economic Growth has conducted a review of training programmes. It looked at over 1 000 evaluations, resulting in the following key findings:

- Many evaluations are not sufficiently robust – only 71 of the evaluations collected met the required standards.
- Training has a positive impact on participant's employment and earnings in more than half of the evaluations reviewed.
- In-firm/on-the-job training programmes outperform classroom based training programmes. Employer co-design and activities that closely mirror actual jobs appear to be key design elements.
- The state of the economy is not a major factor in the performance of training programmes. Programme design features appear to be more important than macroeconomic factors in influencing the success of the programmes examined.

Source: Lamech, S. (2014), "Evidence Strategy: The Danish Approach", http://www.oecd.org/cfe/leed/experts-tackling-disadvantage-paris.htm; OECD (2014d), Job Creation and Local Economic Development, http://dx.doi.org/10.1787/9789264215009-en; What Works Network (2014), https://www.gov.uk/what-works-network.

Better leveraging community assets

Community facilities and assets are not fully utilised

Both Blanchardstown and Meath have significant community assets, and efforts could be strengthened to ensure they are leveraged to the full extent possible.

For example, in Meath, where broadband access is a challenge, schools could serve as a place for the community to access broadband after school hours. While there are a number of benefits to increased use of these facilities (including revenue potential), there are also barriers, including insurance concerns, maintenance, and operation. These issues have the potential to be addressed through the loosening of employment restrictions in certain areas, the use of relevant training and employment programmes, and the use of volunteers. Another example of a social enterprise which is facilitating the use of school and community facilities is provided in Box 5.4.

Box 5.4. Werkhaven and the "key carriers" project

Werkhaven Antwerp is a non profit social economy company, identified as an "EVA" (externally autonomous agency). There are about 320 people working for the organisation. It targets people who have been unemployed for more than one year, have a low degree of education and more than 85% of them have a foreign origin.

The "key carriers" project is an innovative activity, which, above all, brings together workers from the target groups and citizens. Individuals and organisations can ask the city's "Living Together" department for a meeting room in a public building for work or personal functions. The department suggests a meeting room and the user can rely on a "key carrier" of Werkhaven to open and close the room. Under this programme, a school for example, does not need to keep staff working in order to open and close the college gym for a sports association. Besides opening and closing, the key carriers have an important role in logistical support and social control. They help by organising the room, setting up chairs, making coffee and keeping an eye on the way the rooms are left for the next day or group.

Taking into account all these tasks, the key carriers have a big responsibility and need to have a specific profile. Presently, there are more than 50 rooms managed under this programme, which all have their own access modalities and properties. Key carriers must be flexible, customer friendly and independent. Many older workers participate in the programme, which reflects the situation in Flanders where older workers have fewer opportunities in the regular labour market and are consequently the ideal key carriers.

Source: OECD (2015c), *Employment and Skills Strategies in Flanders, Belgium*, OECD Reviews on Local Job Creation. http://dx.doi.org/10.1787/9789264228740-en.

Encouraging asset transfers to social enterprises, charities and other community-based organisations is another potential approach to asset-based community development. Box 5.5 provides an example of a social enterprise in Poland, which has adapted existing community assets for new models. Ireland could also, for example, follow the UK's "right to bid" model. Asset-based development has been aided in the UK by primary legislation in the recent Localism Act which gives communities a "right to bid" by pausing the sale of any community asset before they are disposed of in the open market. These assets can include schools, health buildings, pubs and shops, as well as land. The asset must be listed as a community asset, and can be from the public or private sector, so private assets such as shops or pubs fall under the "right to bid". The Community has six months to prepare a bid once an appeal is upheld. There have been 1 700 "right to bid" applications made in the two years since this right was introduced. This would both help to preserve local services in areas where there is low overall demand, while also supporting community meeting points that can reduce isolation and provide opportunities for networking (so-called "organised proximity").

Box 5.5. Off Piotrkowska

The *Off Piotrkowska* concept was created in 2011 in Poland. The OPG Orange Property Group developed the idea and now co-ordinate it. Because of the economic crisis, business plans to turn a former factory into a modern hotel and office building were suspended. Instead of paying the city of Łódź fines for halting implementation of the investment, OPG Orange Property Group decided to help tenants to start up their own operations. They did this by offering low rent, renovation of the adjacent areas, and joint promotion of all the tenant's activities under the logo "Off Piotrkowska". Most of the tenants are young designers and entrepreneurs focused on the production of clothing and jewellery in small batches. The products are characterised by unique patterns and by a significant proportion of hand-made elements (e.g. *Pan tunie* stał – "You didn't stay here", one of the most popular brands of youth's clothing). By the second half of 2012, some restaurants (predominantly providing ethnic food) and pubs had opened in the area.

Source: OECD (2013a), Demographic transition and an ageing society: Implications for local labour markets in Poland. http://www.oecd.org/cfe/leed/Demographic_poland_report.pdf.

Finally, in developing new community facilities, attention should be paid to how to make sure they are leveraged to the full extent possible. For example, in Meath, the development of mobile facilities could enhance service delivery. In Portugal, the "Net on Wheels" project provides vans with computers, internet access, and professional training to better reach marginalised groups, while Western Economic Diversification (WD) in Canada also facilitates professional skill building initiatives (e.g. auto service, carpentry, electrical, machining, pipe-fitting, plumbing, and welding) through the use of mobile labs (two 55-foot trailers) and e-distance learning (OECD and German Ministry of Food, Agriculture, and Consumer Protection, 2008). "Pooling" services – including both public and private – in one location is another approach to maximising the use of a facility in rural areas. Australia's Rural Transaction Centres bring together a variety of services in one location in towns of less than 3 000 residents, ranging from banking to postal to medicare. In Finland, Citizen Service Offices likewise bring together public, private and non-profit services in a single location (OECD, 2010c).

There are underutilised policy levers to support asset-based development

Particularly in Blanchardstown, there are a large number of private sector actors in the area, yet their engagement with the more disadvantaged areas and communities has not yet reached its full potential. Further efforts could be taken to explore how private actors can be better engaged in supporting local communities in meaningful ways. Ongoing work to improve links with employers in the area, especially with regard to providing work experience for young people who have never worked before and through the Blanchardstown Employer Forum, represent important bases to build on. Employers who have engaged in the JobsPlus programme, for example, have generally found this to be a positive experience. However, overall, there is a recognised need, on the part of both the relevant public services and employers, to strengthen these links and overcome ongoing barriers (information provision, the rules of various employment schemes, etc.) (See section 3 in this chapter for more information). Employers, on their part, could better look to the wider community through their corporate social responsibility programmes and engage in a more sustained way with the local communities.

Several strategies can help encourage local employers to ensure that they offer work experience and recruitment opportunities to local people, including both "carrots" such as tax relief and branding (e.g. "I'm a local employer") and "sticks" such as planning agreements (this could, for example, make planning permission dependent on apprenticeship and internship positions for local residents).

Public procurement can also be used to support the inclusion of local residents in public and not-for-profit services and offer training and apprenticeships. Such social clauses should be considered where projects are of an appropriate nature and scale to allow their use. This issue could be addressed by the Irish Office of Government Procurement (OGP). The OGP was set up in 2014, and together with four key sectors (defence, education, health and local government), is taking responsibility for sourcing all goods and services on behalf of the public service. The OGP is putting in place contracts and framework agreements for public bodies to buy goods and services. It has responsibility for procurement policy and procedures, as well as analytics and data management.

As mentioned in Chapter 2, a few experiments in this regard are already underway in Ireland. For example, Grangegorman DIT and the schools programme used public procurement to hire locally off the live register. Other examples can be found internationally. For example, Nantes, in France, is a municipality playing a leading role in using public procurement to help disadvantaged residents access local employment opportunities, including through social enterprises.

Box 5.6. Intermediate labour markets and private sector-led schemes: Tesco, Seacroft (Leeds) and Dragonville (Durham) Retail creating local jobs

Tesco is the UK's largest retailer and a major contributor to the UK economy. They employ over 200 000 people and create around 10 000 new jobs in the UK every year. 90% of developments are on brownfield sites. When Tesco announced that they were to open a flagship "Extra" store in Seacroft, with the creation of approximately 350 jobs, they knew that the majority of the store's staff was likely to come from within a mile of the store. They realised that in a tightening labour market (Leeds is a rapidly growing retail centre with new developments and major store openings throughout the city), they were unlikely to attract and retain workers from other parts of the city. The local authority's planning processes also required a focus on local employment and enterprise in order to get permission to build the store in the favoured location.

The resulting partnership with a range of statutory and community groups involved the creation of a year-long training programme for unemployed local residents with guaranteed interviews and jobs at the end. The Seacroft Partnership in Leeds has been a highly successful venture. It has involved a wide range of major partners: Leeds City Council; the East Leeds Family Learning Centre; the Employment Service; USDAW (the UK's major retail trade union); and a group of local employers led by Tesco. The development also included retail space for other businesses and not just the Tesco store. When the store opened in November 2000, over 240 previously unemployed local people, many of whom had been out of work for more than two years, took nearly two thirds of the jobs available.

Dragonville is a former mining and industrial area situated on the edge of Durham near the A1 motorway. Like Seacroft, it is an area with a high proportion of social housing. The resident population of the Dragonville area in mid-1998 was 2 200 people. But there were only 600 jobs in the area. 16% of the adult population was on Income Support, compared to 7% in Durham as a whole. The area was ranked 332nd most deprived in the country (DETR, 2000).

The Tesco Extra opened in November 2001 with 340 new jobs – 296 of which went to locally unemployed residents. 120 of the unemployed recruits were previously classed as "economically inactive" and excluded as registered job seekers. These are people who were categorised as not looking for work, people who had been claiming Incapacity Benefit and disability allowances, often described as the "very hardest to help".

In both Seacroft and Dragonville these jobs have proved to be sustainable. Not only do large proportions of people succeed in taking up jobs after the pre-employment training (an average of 85% in both stores), they are still in the jobs over six months later. In Seacroft over 90% of recruits remained in the store and in Dragonville over 81%.

Source: Baker, B. (2002), "Whose store is it anyway?", Case study of Race To The Top project, http://www.racetothetop.org/case/case8.htm.

Box 5.7. Procurement model – Nantes, France

The city of Nantes in South West France has been known for 20 years as a leading innovator in using social clauses in public procurement to stimulate local jobs. Over this time, they have developed sophisticated support structures using insertion enterprises to train and prepare the "clients" to help them to get the jobs that have opened up in the private sector.

In 2008, an evaluation showed that 92 000 hours of work had been created for disadvantaged people, benefiting 266 employees. In addition, they had gained:

- 345 000 hours dedicated to insertion (about 200 full time equivalent jobs).
- 183 contract operations containing a social clause.
- 133 enterprises mobilised through these works, of which 39 are in public works and 66 in building construction.
- 483 beneficiaries with an employment contract, of which 41% are young people, 27% long-term unemployed, 13% on unemployment benefit RMI, and 8% people with a disability.
- 75% of beneficiaries were accompanied by a local insertion company (a "work inclusion" social enterprise).

Changes at the national level on laws for procurement have led to considerable progress in awarding contracts by Nantes Metropole and surrounding suburban administrations (Chantenay, Vannes, Doulon, and Malakoff). Works contracts for which social enterprises have been able to provide apprentices and create longer-term work have included swimming pools, roads, bus routes, and a media centre. The types of trades include mason's assistants, carpenters, painters, building workers, pavers, green space maintenance, plumbers, metalwork, plasterboard, and external cleaning.

Source: OECD (2013b), "Innovative Financing and Delivery Mechanisms for Getting the Unemployed into Work", OECD LEED Forum on Partnerships and Local Development Handbook #7.

The potential for social enterprises could be further developed

There are already social enterprises operating in both Blanchardstown and Meath, whose potential could be further expanded to create more job opportunities and to improve service provision. This requires a conducive framework for them to develop, including clarity on their mission and main features. This framework has to be created at national level and supported at local level, in co-ordination with the local stakeholders. As previously mentioned, at local level, support is being provided to social enterprises, especially in Blanchardstown

Developing social enterprise further in Ireland may require a more concerted cross-government approach. In a report presented to its Directing Committee in 2010, the LEED Programme emphasised "*the need for better co-ordination between different divisions of government* and between different jurisdictions as well as *collaboration* with non-government actors and organisations" in enhancing the social economy. The report underlines that:

The social economy is a template for horizontal or distributed governance. It is inherently a horizontal file and cannot be squeezed into a narrow silo framework. The capacity of the social economy to integrate social and economic objectives, to work across sectoral boundaries, (...), provides sufficient evidence to support a strong recommendation that where the social economy, and social enterprises, are on the policy agenda, they must not be reduced to sectoral strategies (Mendell, 2010, OECD, 2013a).

Figure 5.1 presents an "ideal process" of policy formation to create conducive ecosystems for social enterprises, with the aim of reducing information asymmetries and increasing policy coherence and, therefore, greater effectiveness.

Figure 5.1. **A coherent policy-making process for social enterprises**

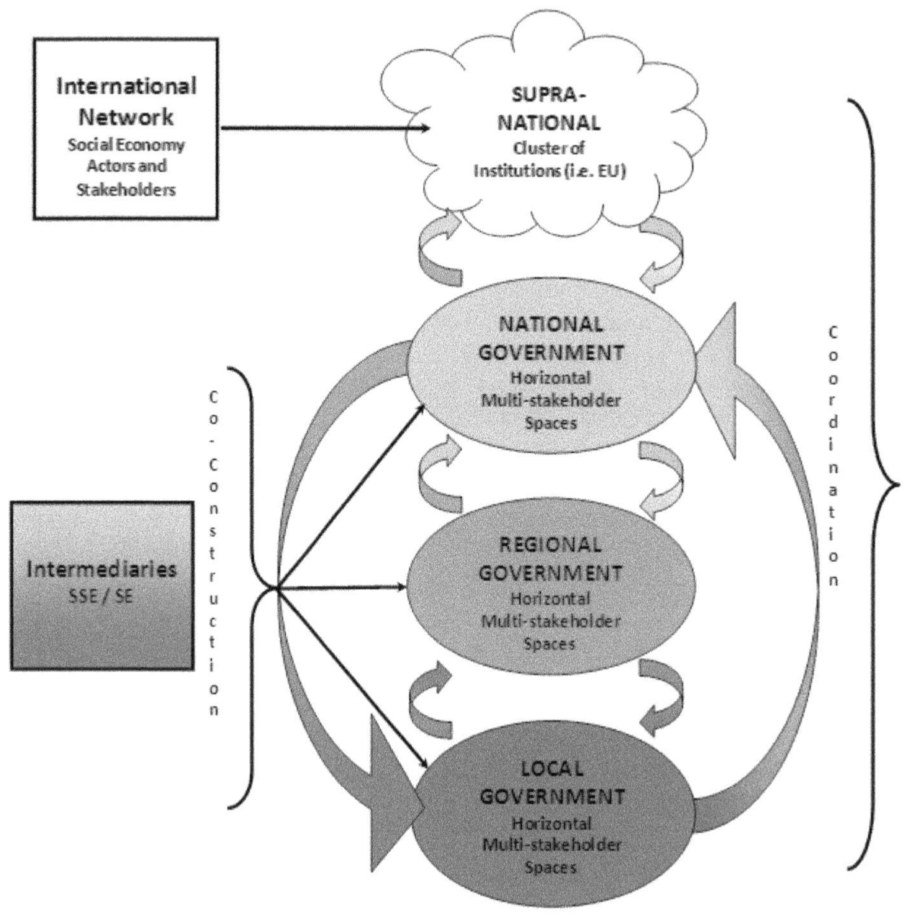

Source: Mendell, M. (2010), "Improving social inclusion at the local level through the social economy: designing an enabling policy framework".

Ireland may be able to learn from an effort to build a conducive ecosystem for social enterprises in Poland. A "Team for Systemic Solutions in the Field of Social Economy" was set up in 2008 bringing together representatives from the government and the social economy. This team, which has been working since its creation towards a tailored enabling environment for social enterprises, has recently drafted the National Strategy for Social Economy Development for the period 2014-2020 (KPRES).

At the national level, a holistic and conducive ecosystem for social enterprises would need to address a number of factors. For one, there is a need to reduce the uncertainty stemming from non-consensual definitions of social enterprise by aligning with the definition of social enterprise used in the EU Social Business Initiative and contextualising it to the Irish landscape of actors, so as to embrace all the different legal entities that can be traced back to the official social enterprise definition. Having such a common definition would allow for more accurate measurement/scoping of the sector.

Adequate supports are also needed to ensure the viability of social enterprise at national and local level, especially in disadvantaged areas. Progress is already being made in Blanchardstown. Moreover, promoting social enterprises and social economy development as a priority in the Operational Plans for the new EU structural funds programming period, promoting innovative financial mechanisms and partnerships for social enterprises, and developing a more conducive financial social market for social enterprises tailored to the needs of these businesses, are important steps to be undertaken or consolidate. Agencies at the national and sub-national levels could do more to support social enterprise development. For example, the recent establishment of the new Local Enterprise Offices (LEOs), which will deliver an improved system of local enterprise supports to start-ups and small businesses across the country, could represent a good opportunity to reach out and to work with social enterprises. LEOs could, in fact, co-operate with local area partnerships to provide a braided support structure for social enterprises as one sub-group of a broader set of enterprises. This is in line with what is emerging in some other European countries (Daniele et al, 2009). This would require capacity building for the public officers to deal with the more specific needs of social enterprises.

Finally, as discussed above, the inclusion of social clauses in public procurement, where projects are of an appropriate nature and scale to allow their use, could also help to support the social enterprise sector. Another example refers to a well consolidated and pioneering practice: that of social co-operatives in Italy, see Box 5.8.

An enlightening example also comes from of the city of Split, in Croatia. The Croatian Law on social care puts an obligation on the city authorities and county centres to support social enterprises or similar organisations. This could be an example that Ireland could follow as a pilot in some selected cities awaiting the transposition of the new EU directive on public procurement. This directive does not make it compulsory for member states to reserve contracts for social enterprises, but leaves them free to instruct special procurement procedures targeting social enterprises. Any such pilot would have to ensure strong accountability mechanisms are put in place.

Within each case study area, the key gaps that social enterprises could fill are of a slightly different nature. In Blanchardstown, thanks to the support offered through the Community Employment Programme and the Community Service Programme, work integration social enterprises play an important role in helping more disadvantaged residents develop the skills and experience needed to access the private sector employment available in the area. In north County Meath, on the other hand, social enterprises could play a role in providing services, as well as boosting job creation, for example through the development of green energy opportunities (see page 133 for more information) and emergency food provision for those in most need (see Box 5.10). Appropriate policy support would be beneficial.

Box 5.8. Public contracting and social enterprises in Italy

Public contracting has contributed to the acknowledgment of social enterprises in Italy; in a few cases public contracts were established by public administrations even before Law 381/1991 on social co-operatives was introduced. The process of contracting out the production of social services to social co-operatives increased substantially after the introduction of the law. According to Law 381, co-operatives of both type A (provision of general interest services) and B (re-integration of vulnerable people in the labour market) can stipulate contracts with public bodies for the delivery of services or work integration activities. As regards work-integration social co-operatives, in particular, the law states that public bodies may "in derogation to the law on contract procurement, stipulate agreements with co-operatives undertaking the activities set out in art. 1, section 1, sub-section b) …" The law thus explicitly recognises an affinity of mission between public bodies and social co-operatives, and emphasises the possibility of collaboration between them.

Preferential purchasing has been a key element in the growth of social co-operatives. Preferential relationships were contested by the European Community, but further legislation in 1996 clarified the situation, allowing municipalities to only accept tenders for contracts from organisations meeting certain requirements (minimum requirement on the employment of disadvantaged people). The revised preferential system has been specifically approved by the European Union, provided that contracts fall under a EUR 200 000 threshold.

Source: Borzaga, C. and Galera, G. (2014), "New Trends in the Non-profit Sector in Europe: the Emergence of Social Enterprise", in M. Andreaus, E. Costa and L. Parker (eds.) *Accountability and Social Accounting for Social and Non-profit Organisations*, Edward Elgar.

Box 5.9. City of Split

Since 2012, the City of Split has provided support to non-profit associations in their activities in social care. Public procurement is one of the envisaged modalities of interaction between the City of Split and non-profit organisations. Based on the Law on Social Care (OG 157/13, 152/14), in particular article 122, large cities and county centres are obliged, according to their financial capabilities, to support non-profit associations and voluntary work in social care. The Official Gazette of the City of Split, 22/14, identifies the following modalities whereby non-profit organisations can be supported:

- Funding for projects and programmes of non-profit associations.
- Public procurement procedures and contracts with selected providers (associations) for social service delivery.
- Funding for supporting co-financing of projects funded by the EU (at most 10% of the total association's co-financing costs).

According to the latest data of the Register of Public Procurement Contracts, the City of Split entered into contracts with nine non-profit associations for service delivery over the last three years. Services delivered include: legal and psycho-social help for the victims of violence, psycho-social treatment of perpetrators of violence, psycho-social rehabilitation of alcoholics, home assistance and care, temporary accommodation of addicts, and temporary accommodation of homeless people.

Source: OECD forthcoming (2016), Report on boosting social entrepreneurship and social entreprise creation in Croatia

Box 5.10. Social and solidarity stores (Epiceries solidaires): helping rebuild community ties while providing good quality food for low-income people

Epiceries solidaires are local convenience stores that provide primary and daily goods to low-income populations, such as the working poor, unemployed, and retirees with a low pension, through significantly decreased prices below the regular retail threshold. Apart from the financial relief, epiceries solidaires aim to restore the dignity of the most vulnerable through the decrease of their dependence on charity and their feeling of being indebted, as well as the increase of their self-esteem through participation in social activities, such as cooking lessons, parent-children activities, employment and re-integration workshops, among others.

Access to epiceries solidaires depends on local, socio-economic and family criteria, for example, the number of children or an income level close to the poverty line. The idea is to be able to respond to specific situations, like an unexpected expense, an accident, or sudden unemployment, so that a household does not fall into severe poverty. The duration of using the epicerie solidaire varies from two to three months and may extend up to one year.

These stores are supported by local authorities, organisations such as the Food Bank and the Red Cross, foundations and private companies, through local or national partnerships. It is worth noting that there is a difference between social and solidarity stores depending on the funding source and under which authority the responsibility falls. Social stores are the responsibility of one or several towns and are public-funded, whereas solidarity stores result from individuals or associations grouped together and are cross-funded.

- 500 social and solidarity stores in France.
- Between 120 000 and 170 000 beneficiaries per year.
- On average, a social store caters for 100 households per year.

Source: A.N.D.E.S. (Association Nationale de Développement des Epiceries Solidaires) (n.d.), Social and solidarity stores website, http://www.epiceries-solidaires.org/english.shtml.

One approach that could cross-cut the above suggestions is establishing social innovation pilot zones. For such a zone to work there would need to be a commitment from public sector actors, and in particular from local authorities and local outlets of national agencies, to experiment in the delivery of services in order to make them more effective. This might include: new methods of commissioning, for example the inclusion of social clauses into public contracts, co-design of delivery with social enterprises or the development of payment by results approaches for the third sector; new ways of inter-departmental working to tackle complex problems; new ways of organising finance, for example through combining funds from different departments into a single pot; new ways of involving communities and service users in the design and delivery of services; and new ways of involving the private sector employers of the area.

Increasing accessibility to economic opportunities

Key gaps exist in vocational education and training

In both local case study areas, there is a need to improve access to vocational education and training opportunities, including apprenticeships and pathways into employment. While the government is taking steps to address this, for example through SICAP, a number of issues stand out as particularly important. For one, the limited number of apprenticeship slots available was identified as a gap in both case study regions. An Apprenticeship Council has recently been established, a promising development. It will be important, going forward, for this Council to consider how to expand apprenticeship beyond the traditional trades to service-based occupations and sectors and ensure that pre-apprenticeship schemes are available in more disadvantaged areas.

Much of the career and education guidance that was once available has been cut in recent years, leaving a key gap. Re-investing in career guidance and ensuring outreach to more isolated populations, including those on social housing estates, is critical. Schools could also give greater priority to vocational and professional training routes at an early stage.

Additionally, previous OECD research (2014a) found that career guidance in Ireland generally does not have a regional and local labour market emphasis and there is limited direct contact between schools and the world of work. Box 5.11 provides one example of how local employers can be involved in providing career guidance. This may be particularly relevant in a place like Blanchardstown, which has a high density of local employers.

Going forward, it will be important to ensure that guidance and training responds to the local labour market. For example, in Blanchardstown, the retail sector may be particularly important. The city of Breda in the southern Netherlands may provide a strong example. In this city, a retail service unit for the sector was set up to better manage labour market transitions into the sector, train staff, and improve work organisation and productivity, as well as the sector's image as a place to work. Local work coaches (who place local people into work) also receive training from the national board for the retail trade.

Additionally, intensive support and ongoing support and mentoring, such as those provided under SICAP, may be needed to aid more disconnected youth and adults in completing their training and gaining employment. BladeRunners in Canada (see Box 5.12) provides a strong example. However, this can be challenging to deliver in practice. For example, the Blanchardstown Area Partnership works with the most disadvantaged people in the area such as lone parents, Travellers, people with mental health issues, ex-offenders and drug users. The Department of Social Protection's "activation" programme is proving to be somewhat of a challenge, with 70 people each week sent from Intreo to the Partnership for education and employment support. It may be possible to build on the experience of the Ballymun Youth Guarantee Scheme, which includes elements of assessment, guidance, education and training and has a particular focus on providing a work placement opportunity with local employers (although there have been difficulties in reaching the required work placement targets – see OECD, 2014b).

Box 5.11. Netz der Chancen: career guidance at an early stage

The *Netz der Chancen* is funded by the district authority of *Steglitz-Zehlendorf* in Berlin, through resources of the European Social Funds (ESF) (EUR 248 789). Furthermore, its work is supported by the regional network for vocational training in Steglitz-Zehlendorf. The main aim of the project is to overcome barriers between pupils and businesses and to enable them to engage in active and lively conversations through a regular event called the *Tag der Chancen*. During these events, diverse businesses present themselves, their sector and their training possibilities to pupils from different schools in Steglitz-Zehlendorf. There, pupils get the chance to find out about exciting training possibilities within their own district.

In the first part of the day, the interview phase, trainees from the businesses present the companies they work for and the course of their training. They answer pupils' questions and remarks and describe their own professional development. By sharing their personal experiences and funny anecdotes, they create interesting conversations that lead to a more active participation of the pupils. The setting of the event allows them to speak at eye level, which further diminishes barriers and inhibitions.

The second part of the day consists of a "market of opportunities". In this fair-like environment pupils can directly and individually engage in conversations with businesses, trainees or HR managers, in order to learn more about the training, career opportunities and other important details. It is also during this phase, that trainees present samples of their work, including the pupils in the process. In doing so, they actively learn about the profession and gain experience in a dynamic way. Furthermore, the pupils may acquire so-called Blue Cards, a kind of voucher that businesses can hand out to interesting and suitable pupils. Each company gets to define their own Blue Card terms: it could be the possibility of doing an internship, a trial day or even a direct invitation to a job interview.

So far, seven Tage der Chancen, each with a focus on diverse business sectors, have been organised. Over 700 pupils, from more than 15 schools, actively participated in the project and engaged with trainees and HR managers. Furthermore, approximately 250 representatives from different businesses, technical colleges and education service providers took part in the organised events.

The project's website (www.netz-der-chancen.de) offers interested people the opportunity to have a look at the profiles of participating schools, organisations and businesses. Also, an expert panel on the topic "School and Economy", consisting of teachers and recruiters, has been established.

Source: Bezirkliche Bündnisse für Wirtschaft und Arbeit (n.d.), Local Pacts for Economy and Employment in Berlin. Project Sheet example.

Box 5.12. BladeRunners

BladeRunners is an employment programme that helps youth (ages 15-30) with multiple barriers to employment build careers in construction and other industries, throughout the province of British Columbia (BC), Canada. The Ministry of Jobs, Tourism and Innovation is the lead sponsor of the programme, which is now run in 32 locations across the province by 19 different local service delivery organisations. The BladeRunners programme provides participating youth with a three-week training course, including instruction in both soft and hard skills, and then facilitates direct job placement for programme graduates. The programme also provides extensive support services for participants and graduates 24 hours a day, seven days a week for an undetermined period of time after placement. The ultimate goal of the programme is to develop skills and work experience that foster long-term attachment to the labour force and to support the social and community integration of young people. BladeRunners is widely regarded as a highly effective employment training model for young people with multiple barriers to employment. It advertises an overall 77% post-training job placement rate, has won several awards and recognitions for its achievements, and is funded by a diverse group of public and private supporters.

Source: OECD (2013c), *Local Strategies for Youth Employment*, www.oecd.org/employment/leed/local-strategies-youth-employment.htm.

The Youth Guarantee Implementation Plan provides one avenue for addressing many of the issues described above. The Youth Guarantee, which is part of a Europe-wide initiative, aims to provide young people under the age of 25 with a good quality offer of employment, continued education, an apprenticeship or a traineeship within a short time of becoming unemployed. Various existing schemes have been modified to have a specific focus on young people. In Ireland, the scheme has been piloted in a disadvantaged suburb of north Dublin, adjacent to Blanchardstown, involving extensive use of the local employment services and job clubs. Initial indications are that most of the young people engaged with were offered a relevant opportunity in a timely fashion, and the feedback from the participants themselves as well as from education and training providers, employers and other stakeholders was generally positive. However, difficulties were experienced in getting very marginalised young people jobs in a competitive labour market (Devlin, 2015).

Tweaks may also be needed for existing programmes. For example, a training budget could be established for the Tús programme, ensuring that volunteers are able to access funds for on-the-job training courses. While some stakeholders argue that training should not be an obligatory part of the programme, it could still be useful to put in place a flexible fund that organisations taking on volunteers could access, in order to support progression into employment. It would also be useful to open this programme up to a higher number of people taking the scheme voluntarily, to ensure that it is open to those that genuinely want to build their skills and engagement.

Finally, further work also needs to be done to ensure that "work pays". An ongoing issue of importance in many OECD countries is the need to ensure that people are better off in employment than in receipt of benefit. In Ireland, this relates to factors such as the withdrawal of rent supplement and other benefits when taking up a job, as well as payment of income tax and other taxes and charges. Currently, the system is very complex, as each scheme and initiative has detailed rules. In the United Kingdom, the introduction of a Universal Credit shows some promise in tailing off benefit support more gradually as people go into work and as they go up the salary scale.

Entrepreneurship and SME support could better focus on an area's comparative advantage

Much of the support available for entrepreneurs in Ireland focuses on enterprises with the capacity to export: direct supports (i.e. financial supports) are only available to this type of firm, while others can also access "soft" supports (mentoring, training, etc.).[2] Such policies may leave gaps in supports for enterprises in places like Meath, which may have strong comparative advantage in domestic sector niches or serve adjacent town/city markets. For example, there is the potential to better tap into the Dublin city region market, opportunities in the silver and white economy, given the age profile of the area, and/or potential green energy development.

Harnessing innovation and promoting entrepreneurship in rural areas, such as north County Meath, can be important in supporting greater economic prosperity. As people in rural areas do not have such easy access to solutions and products from outside, they can generate innovative forms of problem solving, and forms of import substitution that could be harnessed and developed. Further new firms can take advantage of lower land and labour costs as they develop and grow. Another important factor is exploring new forms of economic diversification that build on the existing skills sets in the region (see Neffke et al, 2011, and Neffke and Henning, 2013). Identifying such skills sets may require mapping the existing products and services that have traditionally been developed locally and identifying the potential for skills and people to transfer to new types of economic development and industry.

Green energy may provide a particular opportunity that should be explored, particularly as the area is close to Dublin so that storage and transfer for energy could be facilitated. According to the Pobal report *Employment and Social Inclusion in Rural Areas: A Fresh Start* (Walsh and Harvey, 2013), Ireland lags behind other European countries in terms of renewables, organic farming, biomass and nature protection in rural areas, and the report suggests that certain schemes, such as micro-turbines, are particularly effective at using local labour. The development of renewable energy could also bring medium-term income streams to local landowners, or communities, which may also benefit from cheaper energy and grid improvements. Social enterprises can help deliver this agenda.

Local Enterprise Offices (LEOs) provide advice, information, training, mentoring and limited direct financial aid to micro and small enterprises. With more flexibility in how they allocate grants locally, LEOs could provide a greater range of financial supports to micro and small enterprises. Consideration could be given to extension of their remit so that new firms, including social enterprises, would be able to avail of these supports to access local domestic markets, as well as international markets.

Regardless of the comparative advantage exploited, the LEOs could also play a role in supporting networking, sharing resources and pooling, especially in rural areas like north County Meath where entrepreneurs tend to be more isolated, and lack the informal types of knowledge exchange which often develop in cities and larger urban areas. Supporting greater networking within the existing rural business sector could nurture and extend the scope of "organised proximity" (Copus et al, 2011) and increase the opportunities for the sharing of new innovations, and the development of new regional co-operation and brands. LEOs can play a role in increasing market intelligence, building regional brands, and making more strategic attempts to identify and better exploit comparative advantage. The work of the Networks (ACEnet) in rural Ohio Central Appalachian Network (CAN) provides one example of how this can be done.

Box 5.13. The Central Appalachian Network (CAN)

The Central Appalachian region is a mountainous area that extends over parts of the five states of Kentucky, Ohio, Tennessee, Virginia, and West Virginia and includes some of the most economically distressed communities in the United States. Since 1993, the Central Appalachian Network (CAN) has been focused on building a healthy and sustainable regional economy through ecologically sustainable rural development strategies. CAN comprises eight non-profit institutions and organisations, and with funding support from the W.K. Kellogg Foundation and the Appalachian Regional Commission, a joint Federal-13 state regional development agency, has formulated a set of sustainable entrepreneurship strategies, based on the network's practical experiences and research from across the country. CAN has identified a number of strategies, including the following:

- **Build on Appalachia's assets.** Asset-based entrepreneurship is based on the sustainable use of forests, farmland, rivers, lakes, and mountains, through products such as organic and niche crops, ecotourism, and wood products from sustainably harvested timber, all drawing from the beauty and heritage of the region, including traditional crafts, music, foods and architecture. Asset-based entrepreneurship is a major contributor to the regional economy and is growing annually. The natural assets are seen as the region's competitive advantage. Programmes include helping entrepreneurs identify and develop niche markets, expanding market power through regional marketing, and focusing on improving the quality and quantity of products and services.
- **Regional Markets for Rural Entrepreneurs.** CAN promotes regional clusters as an economic development strategy. These are informal geographic concentrations of entrepreneurs, specialised suppliers, service providers, trade associations, regional development agencies, universities and governments who serve similar markets and collaborate for mutual gain. In the Central Appalachian region, clusters have been promoted and supported by incubators (kitchens, arts, wood products), technical institutions, and specialised infrastructure, such as solar wood-drying kilns, with the aim of spurring innovations, improving quality, reducing business set-up costs, and expanding markets.

Source: Dabson, B. (2006), "Central Appalachian Network (CAN): Strategies for Sustainable Entrepreneurship in Appalachia, U.S." Discussion paper for Entrepreneurship in the Districts Uckermark (Brandenburg) and Parchim (Mecklenburg-Western Pomerania), http://www.oecd.org/cfe/leed/37963087.pdf.

Improve early years education and care, family services and community development

Good quality early years education and care enhances the future for all children, but is especially important for children from disadvantaged backgrounds to ensure they get a good start in life. The need to improve access to early education and care, and ensure its quality, is a national issue in Ireland, and was particularly evident in the two case study areas of Blanchardstown and north County Meath. Challenges are varied: for people who need childcare the issue is the availability and cost of the provision, especially when trying to access work or to maintain work in relatively low paid jobs; for providers, especially in rural areas, it is the challenge of providing childcare at affordable prices while maintaining standards; while for childcare workers it is low wage rates along with limited opportunities for career progression.

The provision of affordable, flexible, high quality childcare and out of school care needs to be appropriate given the needs of children and their parents. This requires additional investment in early education, through schemes such as the Community Childcare Subvention, the Childcare Employment and Training Support Scheme, and the Free Pre-School Year, or the amalgamation of some or all of these schemes into one scheme or fund.

The quality of early years education and care needs to be age-appropriate and of a good standard. This is important for all children, but especially for children from disadvantaged backgrounds and for children with special needs. For this to happen, there is a need for adherence to certain standards, along with support for providers, and inspections to ensure quality criteria are being met.

A critical part of the provision of good quality early years education and care is a well-qualified and adequately paid workforce. This requires support for childcare workers and early years educators to have certain levels of qualifications and for there to be opportunities for career progression, along with a progressive pay structure. Investment will be required to develop and support this, especially to ensure the availability of affordable quality early years education and care provision in disadvantaged areas.

Recent developments in Ireland are promising in this regard. An Inter-Departmental Group on Future Investment in Child Care, which reported in July 2015, identified and assessed options for improving the affordability, quality and supply of early years and school-age childcare (Inter-Departmental Working Group, 2015). Further recent developments include an extension to the free pre-school so that every child in Ireland will be able to start school at the age of three, and remain in pre-school until they start primary school. There are also additional supports to enable children with disabilities to fully participate in pre-school education, as well as a number of measures to improve the quality of childcare provision in general. Additional places have been provided on the Community Childcare Subvention programme to assist low-income families, and work is in hand to develop a single programme of affordable childcare to replace the existing schemes.[3]

Evidence from the case studies also showed the importance of supporting vulnerable families and their communities in addressing disadvantages and in preparing individuals to avail of opportunities to improve their livelihoods. These supports are required in the areas of health, especially mental health, through personal and community development and through addressing issues associated with the use of illegal drugs. For many of the families in the case study areas, these issues need to be dealt with before they are in a position to take up education and training opportunities or to move into employment.

This calls for the acknowledgement of health needs and the provision of adequate health services in conjunction with other services. In Blanchardstown, there are health services available, including the provision of community mental health services. These service providers need to be working with the other service providers in the area, such as education services, employment support programmes and employers to ensure a holistic approach to supporting people who are unemployed and have multiple needs. In north County Meath, access to such services is an issue, especially for younger people. There are health services provided at the retirement village in Kilmainhamwood, but for many others they may have to travel to Navan to access such services, and may be reluctant to do so for cost reasons.

The importance of personal and community development is widely acknowledged as important to building skills and confidence in disadvantaged families and communities. Yet, because of the economic crisis, many community development services have been reduced in disadvantaged areas. There is a need to reconsider the value of such services in giving people a start and providing much needed support in improving their lives and in invigorating their communities. For this reason, consideration should be given to supporting community development in areas where a need for such support has been identified, such as in the Blanchardstown RAPID area and in north County Meath. While there are existing community initiatives in these areas, there is evidence of the need for further support and stimuli.

Illegal drug use and associated criminality was evident in Blanchardstown and, while less obvious, was also an issue raised in north County Meath, especially in relation to some young people in the villages of Kilmainhamwood and Drumconrath. While the drugs task force and associated initiatives have tackled many aspects of the problem in Blanchardstown, it has not been eliminated. At times of recession, with limited job opportunities and high levels of unemployment, people can be attracted to illegal drug taking and associated activities, where there are seen to be few alternatives. Thus, it is important that alternatives are provided and that treatment is available for those who wish to avail of it.

Improve systems for migrant integration

Better support for the social and economic integration of immigrant communities is a clear priority, especially for areas such as Blanchardstown. One key gap appears to be the provision of English language classes. Education and training boards are currently responsible for providing ESOL and EFL courses, but due to concerns around the adequacy of the provision, a number of bottom-up initiatives have emerged to supplement this provision. A more co-ordinated strategy for English language training is needed, including ensuring that it is tailored to individual needs, is offered at times that are both "work friendly" and "family friendly" and including specific training in workplace language skills and vocabulary (for example, in construction trades). Social enterprises may also be able to play a role here. While proficiency in the English language is a requirement for most jobseekers in getting a job, there is also a need for more translation of materials on websites into key languages and ensuring that mainstream services pay for interpretation services when dealing with families to avoid relying on children as interpreters (e.g. health, housing, social services).

The Irish Government is in the process of preparing a migrant integration strategy, following a period of consultation. The migrant integration strategy will address issues such as: promoting cultural awareness and combating racism and xenophobia; education; social inclusion and access to public services; employment and pathways to work; and active citizenship. Development of the strategy involves a number of government departments along with input from a migrant consultative forum.

Other OECD countries have adopted a model of "one-stop shop" centres to support the integration of migrants, such as the National Immigrant Support Centres in Portugal. Such one-stop shops provide one-to-one advice on a range of migrant issues, run interpretation services and also provide community development work around common issues. Key to their success is finding ways to engage migrants themselves as leaders and staff, so that local migrant networks can be "tapped into" in a productive way. While this represents one model for better integrating services, given the resource constraints in launching a new centre, consideration could also be given to how existing agencies could work more effectively together, through, for example, providing joint outreach services.

Box 5.14. National Immigrant Support Centres, Lisbon and Porto, Portugal

In 2004, in Portugal, the High Commission for Immigration and Intercultural Dialogue (ACIDI) developed two one-stop shops, called National Immigrant Support Centres (CNAIs), in Lisbon and Porto. These two centres, created exclusively for immigration issues, bring together under the same roof a number of services related to immigration. Through shared responsibility and partnership between various levels of the Portuguese Government, the centres involve six branches of five Ministries (Foreigners and Borders Service, Working Conditions Authority, Social Security, Central Registry Office, Health and Education) and offices that provide specific support with regard to legal advice, family re-unification and labour market integration, among other issues.

The services are enhanced through the involvement of more than 80 cultural mediators from the different immigrant communities. These stakeholders, representing immigrant associations and working in partnership with the government, have a key role as a bridge between the immigrants and Portuguese public administration.

In 2006, the International Organization for Migration (IOM) undertook an independent evaluation of the outcomes of these support centres. The evaluation concluded that the National Immigrant Support Centre model "is an effective initiative and an experience that should be disseminated, and that can be internationally replicated within other institutional contexts".

The one-stop shops are only part of the ACIDI services. They also provide web and telephone services to migrants across the country, through a series of platforms for social emergencies, employment, health, benefits, enterprise and entrepreneurship, and accreditation of foreign qualifications. Through this work, they also sensitise the mainstream service providers to the needs of immigrants and provide inter-cultural training to front-line staff.

Source: Abranches, Maria (2009), "Evaluation of the National Immigrant Support Services in Portugal". http://www.unaoc.org/ibis/wp-content/uploads/2010/05/Integration-Services-in-Portugal-Evaluation-Report-English-Version.pdf

The built environment also plays an important role in facilitating, or inhibiting, access

The concentration of social housing and poor quality private sector stock in Blanchardstown provides affordable housing to many different people (including new immigrants), but it needs to be further investigated whether this area is acting as a springboard to higher value housing and jobs in the Dublin city-region (providing social mobility) or whether it leads to people becoming more isolated from economic activity, and unable to move, thereby contributing to inter-generational disadvantage. Robson et al. (2008) analysed relatively deprived areas in the United Kingdom and identified four types of neighbourhood: "transit"; "escalator"; "improver"; and "isolated". While some neighbourhoods show more dynamism as people move in and out of them, others are more likely to "trap people in space". The Australian Housing and Urban Research Institute AHURI (Hulse and Pinnegar, 2015) argues that a focus on "mobilities" (in terms of both the daily commute, social and occupational mobility and longer-term housing mobility over the lifetime) is particularly important in understanding the link between the housing market and relative poverty. They argue that mobility is itself a resource.

It will be important to better measure the relative isolation of this housing from appropriate employment opportunities, whether there are sufficient low-skilled jobs to meet needs locally, and if not, whether there is sufficient accessibility to get to such jobs elsewhere in Dublin, and at a cost which will "make work pay". Centre for Cities in the UK has recently identified strong discrepancies between where lower income people are living in UK cities and where concentrations of lower skilled jobs are found, leading to considerable mobility constraints (Tochtermann and Clayton, 2011). The situation is exacerbated because lower skilled jobs do not always pay the wages required to cover transport costs. The analysis indicates that over 70% of lower skilled residents live in local authority districts with fewer jobs than residents already in or looking for work.

Interestingly, AHURI found that the most important element in improving social mobility and life chances was ensuring that people were living in safe and secure communities with an absence of crime and anti-social behaviour. It is clear from the space syntax analysis carried out for this report that spatial layouts of social housing estates are not serving residents well, and may be exacerbating crime and anti-social behaviour in both Blanchardstown and Meath.

Nevertheless, the Irish Government currently has a commitment to building sustainable communities. The importance of integrating services is central to the core concept of the National Spatial Strategy, and its successor, the National Planning Framework. In addition, the Department of Housing, Planning, Community and Local Government has produced design guidelines which set out the principles and criteria that are important in the design of housing in order to facilitate the delivery of better homes, better neighbourhoods and better urban spaces. A range of design priorities are emphasised to ensure designs are socially, environmentally and architecturally appropriate, safe, secure and healthy.[4]

Therefore, it is important that the current investment in social housing in Ireland pays attention to these principles of good design (such as ensuring strong "natural surveillance", and the regular "through-movement" of non-residents) that are now applied in many OECD countries (see Box 5.15).

Box 5.15. Urban design as a tool for promotion of lively and safe local communities: international examples

There are useful international examples of the use of urban design and space syntax techniques to create regional amenities, such as shopping centres, that are also locally accessible and give a boost to the urban fabric. Further space syntax techniques are also being used to help create safer communities.

In **the City of Gosnells, in Perth**, Australia there were strong concerns about local community safety leading to a Safer City Initiative. Many local authorities in the Perth region had opted for expensive city patrols. However, Gosnells elected to go for a mixed strategy, with 30 different programmes including youth projects, lighting programmes, and focused public interventions in particular crime spot areas, such as parks. For example, in parks patrols were supplemented with intervention and mentoring programmes, significantly lowering local crime and anti-social behaviour rates. The city also incorporated an environmental re-design element, using space syntax techniques to identify the spatial location of crimes, and to identify local movement patterns. The City Designer identified that much of the local estates had been designed on the basis of creating "defensible space" (first conceptualised by Oscar Newman) on the assumption that quieter areas that were isolated from the movement of strangers would be safer. In fact, space syntax analysis showed that it was the streets without much pedestrian movement, and those with low visibility from passers by (for example due to the construction of high walls) that were the most vulnerable to crime. In order to address this issue, the new policies include a more accessible street network, ensuring that community and retail facilities are on streets and paths with high rates of movement, and ensuring that all local amenities were accessible by foot, increasing pedestrian movement. The aim is to decrease crime by 10% in three years (2014-17). For more information, see http://www.gosnells.wa.gov.au/Your_property/Community_safety/Safe_City_initiative/Designing_out_crime

In **Melrose Arch, Greater Johannesburg**, South Africa, an original plan to develop a shopping mall with 18 hectares of land was abandoned in favour of developing a set of dense mixed use streets that would create a more lively urban fabric – what one of the main investors identified as "building town". The project formed an important part of the Greater Johannesburg Metropolitan Council's development strategy. The aim was to create a development that was both globally attractive (bringing in people from outside areas) and locally accessible. Initially, this was seen as a risky strategy, as high rates of violence had caused some to "bunker down", leading to the development of very separate and isolated zoned land uses. The final layout includes a new inter-connected network of streets, a tree-lined boulevard, a main street and two new urban squares. The main street has retail on the ground floor, commercial office space above, and residential above that. While the development is particularly porous and open, bringing public transport up the boulevard, the influx of people it has attracted provides a form of "natural surveillance". The development is a commercial success and is seen as an example of the triumph of "urbanism over architecture". For more information, see http://www.arup.com/Projects/Melrose_Arch.aspx

Source: Compiled by Space Syntax Ltd.

Immediate priorities for action

The findings from this study point to a wide range of actions that can be taken across policy areas to better promote inclusive growth and tackle disadvantage in Ireland. However, given that Ireland is currently implementing or has already implemented a number of recent reforms, it is unrealistic to expect such a broad range of actions to be taken simultaneously. Therefore, a number of immediate priorities have been identified, based both on their relative importance and their feasibility for implementation given the current policy environment. These priorities are summarised in the Box 5.16. In addition to priorities at the national level, a number of priorities for each local case study are also identified.

Box 5.16. Immediate priorities for action

Improving governance and building capacities

- **Enhance an integrated services approach.** Ireland has already taken significant steps to better integrate and co-ordinate services (e.g. establishment of Intreo and LCDCs amongst other reforms). Particular attention should be paid to how to address disadvantage at a very local level (i.e. in the "pockets" of extreme disadvantage), as more mainstream reforms on their own may not be sufficient to catalyse broader change in such communities, and may need to be complemented by locally targeted efforts.
- **Build capacities at the local level.** Local actors are now being asked to take on new responsibilities (e.g. through the LCDCs). Coupled with a diminishment in capacities at the local level, as a result of the crisis, (e.g. due to the freeze in public sector hiring from 2009-2014), a clear need for building local skills and capacities exists.
- **Establish a "what works centre".** Both national and local actors could benefit from having a stronger understanding of programme impacts and best practices. An independent "what works centre" could play an important role in collecting and collating evaluation evidence, as well as building an evidence-based policy culture.

Better leveraging of community assets

- **Support social enterprises.** Establish a conducive ecosystem for social enterprises through a co-ordinated and co-operative approach at national and sub-national level. This includes: providing an appropriate legislative and regulatory framework; tailoring public procurement to foster the delivery of social services by promoting social clauses; facilitating access to finance; and providing capacity building opportunities to social enterprises. These efforts can complement other efforts to develop and utilise other types of community assets (voluntary associations, local schools, etc.)

Box 5.16. Immediate priorities for action *(Continued)*

Increasing accessibility to economic opportunity

- **Strengthen career guidance.** Career guidance plays an important role in helping young people develop sustainable career pathways, and the current limited provision could have longer-term implications for the labour market. In re-investing in career guidance, attention should be paid to making it responsive to local and regional labour markets, as well as ensuring its provision both in and outside of schools.
- **Expand and improve apprenticeship offerings.** Work in this area is already underway through the newly established Apprenticeship Council. Going forward, it will be important for this council to consider how to expand apprenticeships to non-traditional sectors, as well as how to make them accessible to disadvantaged populations, including through the provision of pre-apprenticeships and wrap-around support.
- **Improve co-ordination of migrant integration services to reduce gaps and duplication.** The co-ordination of a range of services for migrants in local communities can play a critical role in improving migrant integration. Cultural sensitivity and building authentic linkages with migrant communities will be key in making such initiatives successful. Such initiatives could bring together different services in existing facilities, such as schools, and/or consist of joined up outreach carried out by different agencies in tandem. The current development of a National Migrant Integration Strategy represents a potential avenue for addressing these issues.
- **Invest in early years education and care.** Ensuring provision is age-appropriate and of a good standard requires a well-qualified and well-paid work force, as well as targeted support for disadvantaged children and their families.

Blanchardstown RAPID Area

- **Use a broker to stimulate better sign-posting between local services.** In a "crowded platform" such as Blanchardstown, further co-ordination of existing services is just as critical as bringing in new services. A dedicated broker can help in this regard.
- **Intensify ongoing efforts to encourage employers to engage more with local residents.** There are important ongoing efforts to engage the large number of local employers, but more work could be done to intensify their role in providing training and employment opportunities for local residents, particularly those from disadvantaged communities.
- **Consider the development of a local training facility**, or improve access to facilities which can provide training in the local area.
- **Further consolidate a strategy for social enterprises**, especially those that focus on work integration of vulnerable people.

North County Meath

- **Consider how to better leverage community facilities.** Attention should be paid to how existing community facilities can serve a broader range of community needs, as well as how the development of new assets, such as mobile outreach and training centres, can better serve the community.
- **Identify and build on local comparative advantages.** In developing the local economy, more attention is needed on how to build on local comparative advantages, such as the proximity to Dublin or the potential for green energy development.
- **Establish a strategy for social enterprises** that focuses on job creation and provision of social services.
- **Address communication and access limitations** through improved broadband provision and better transport links.

Notes

1. See http://www.socialinclusion.ie/pia.html for more information
2. https://www.localenterprise.ie/Documents-and-Publications/Entrepreneurship-in-Ireland-2014.pdf
3. The existing schemes are: Community Childcare Subvention (CCS), Training and Employment Childcare Programmes (TEC), comprising After-School Childcare (ASCC), Childcare Education and Training Support (CETS) and Community Employment Childcare (CEC).
4. It is noted that, in Ireland, the instrument for the regulation and control of development is the Development Plan. The public can make submissions or observations, within specified time periods, on what is being proposed by the planning authority when the plan is being developed.

References

A.N.D.E.S. (Association Nationale de Développement des Epiceries Solidaires) (n.d.), Social and solidarity stores website, http://www.epiceries-solidaires.org/english.shtml.

Abranches, Maria. (2009). "Evaluation of the National Immigrant Support Services in Portugal". International Organization for Migration, Lisbon. http://www.unaoc.org/ibis/wp-content/uploads/2010/05/Integration-Services-in-Portugal-Evaluation-Report-English-Version.pdf.

AIRO, Dublin City Council Housing Monitoring Tool, http://dublindashboard.ie/pages/MappedDublinRegionHousing

Baker, B. (2002), "Whose store is it anyway?", *Case study of Race To The Top project*, http://www.racetothetop.org/case/case8.htm

Bezirkliche Bündnisse für Wirtschaft und Arbeit (n.d.), Local Pacts for Economy and Employment in Berlin. Project Sheet example.

Bookle, S. (2013), "Final Report of the Demographic Profile of Mulhuddart-Dublin 15", Burtenshaw Kenny Associates, Dublin.

Bookle, S. (2012), "Final Report: Blanchardstown RAPID AIT", Burtenshaw Kenny Associates, Dublin.

Borzaga, C. and Galera, G. (2014), "New Trends in the Non-profit Sector in Europe: the Emergence of Social Enterprise", in M. Andreaus, E. Costa and L. Parker (eds.) *Accountability and Social Accounting for Social and Non-profit Organisations*, Edward Elgar.

Central Statistics Office (2015a), *Survey on Income and Living Conditions* (SILC) 2013, www.cso.ie.

Central Statistics Office (2015b), *Quarterly National Household Survey: Quarter 3 2015*, www.cso.ie.

Central Statistics Office (2015c), *Measuring Ireland's Progress 2013*. www.cso.ie.

Central Statistics Office (2015d), *County Incomes and Regional GDP: 2012*, CSO, Dublin.

Central Statistics Office (2015e), *Quarterly National Household Survey: QNHS Households and Family Units Quarter 2 2009 – Quarter 2 2015*, CSO, Dublin, www.cso.ie.

Central Statistics Office (2015f), *Survey on Income and Living Conditions (SILC) 2014 results*, www.cso.ie.

Central Statistics Office (2014a), *Survey on Income and Living Conditions (SILC) 2012*, CSO, Dublin.

Central Statistics Office (2014b), *County Incomes and Regional GDP: 2011*, CSO, Dublin.

Central Statistics Office (2014c), *Quarterly National Household Survey: Quarter 2 2014*, CSO, Dublin www.cso.ie.

Central Statistics Office (2013a), *Statistical Yearbook of Ireland.*, CSO, Dublin.

Central Statistics Office (2013b), *Quarterly National Household Survey: Quarter 4 2012*, Dublin: CSO.

Central Statistics Office (2012), *This is Ireland: Highlights from the Census 2011, Part 1.* CSO, Dublin.

Central Statistics Office (2011), *Census 2011 Results: Area Profiles for Towns*, CSO, Dublin.

Central Statistics Office (2011), *Census 2011 Small Area Population Statistics* (SAP) at http://census.cso.ie/sapmap/

Central Statistics Office (2007), *Quarterly National Household Survey: Quarter 3 2007*, CSO, Dublin.

Cingano, F. (2014), "Trends in Income Inequality and its Impact on Economic Growth", OECD Social, Employment and Migration Working Papers, No. 163, OECD Publishing, Paris. http://dx.doi.org/10.1787/5jxrjncwxv6j-en

Commission for the Economic Development of Rural Areas (2013), "Energising Ireland's Rural Economy", www.ruralireland.ie.

Copus, A.K., Shucksmith, M., Dax, T. and Meredith, D. (2011): Cohesion Policy for rural areas after 2013: A rationale derived from the EDORA project (European Development Opportunities in Rural Areas) - ESPON 2013 Project 2013/1/2. Studies in Agricultural Economics 113 (2), 121-132.

Dabson, B. (2006), "Central Appalachian Network (CAN): Strategies for Sustainable Entrepreneurship in Appalachia, U.S." Discussion paper for Entrepreneurship in the Districts Uckermark (Brandenburg) and Parchim (Mecklenburg-Western Pomerania), OECD LEED Programme, http://www.oecd.org/cfe/leed/37963087.pdf

Daniele, D., T. Johnson and F. Zandonai (2009), "Networks as Support Structures for Social Enterprises", in *The Changing Boundaries of Social Enterprises*, OECD Publishing, Paris. http://dx.doi.org/10.1787/9789264055513-5-en

Department of Agriculture, Food and the Marine (2014), "Ireland's Draft Rural Development Programme 2014-202: Summary of Draft Measures", www.agriculture.gov.ie/ruralenvironment/draftruraldevelopmentprogramme2014-2020.

Department of Children and Youth Affairs (2015) *Blueprint for the Development of Children and Young People's Services Committees.* Dublin: Department of Children and Youth Affairs. Available at www.dcya.ie.

Department of Social Protection (2015), *Statistical Information on Social Welfare Services 2014*, www.welfare.ie.

Department of Social Protection (2014), "Ireland: National Social Report 2014", http://www.welfare.ie/en/Pages/Ireland-National-Social-Report-2014.aspx.

Department of the Taoiseach (2015), "National Reform Programme: Ireland", http://www.taoiseach.gov.ie/eng/Publications/Publications_2015/National_Reform_Programme_2015.html.

Department of the Taoiseach (2014), "National Reform Programme: Ireland", http://www.taoiseach.gov.ie/eng/Publications/Publications_2014/National_Reform_Programme_2014.html.

DETR (Department of the Environment, Transport and the Regions) (2000), "Indices of Deprivation 2000: Regeneration", Research Summary, No. 31.Devlin, D. (2015) Key learning from the Ballymun Youth Guarantee Project. Policy and Practice Report. Dublin: Department of Social Protection.

Devlin, M. (2015) Key Learning from the Ballymun Youth Guarantee Project. Dublin: Department of Social Protection.

Dufty-Jones, R. (2012), "Moving home: theorizing housing within a politics of mobility", Housing, Theory and Society, 29(2), 207-222.

Elvidge, J. (2014), "A Route Map to an Enabling State", Scotland: Carnegie UK Trus www.carnegieuktrust.org.uk.

European Commission (2014), "A Map of social enterprises and their eco-systems in Europe Country Report: Ireland", prepared by ICF Consulting Services, http://ec.europa.eu/social/BlobServlet?docId=13028&langId=en .

Eurostat (2015), Employment and unemployment (LFS), http://ec.europa.eu/eurostat/web/lfs/data.

EXODEA Europe (2009), "Joining up the Dots …. Study of Employment Opportunities Arising from Grangegorman Development in Dublin's North Inner City", https://www.dit.ie/media/grangegorman/documents/Employment%20Study.pdf.

Forfás (2013), "Social Enterprise in Ireland: Sectoral Opportunities and Policy Issues", http://www.forfas.ie/media/23072013-Social_Enterprise_in_Ireland_Publcation.pdf.

Friedrich, E., Hillier, B., & Chiaradia, A. (2009). "Anti-social behaviour and urban configuration using space syntax to understand spatial patterns of socio-environmental disorder", Proceedings of the 7th International Space Syntax Symposium, http://discovery.ucl.ac.uk/18582/1/18582.pdf.

Froy, F. et al. (2011), "Building Flexibility and Accountability Into Local Employment Services: Synthesis of OECD Studies in Belgium, Canada, Denmark and the Netherlands", OECD Local Economic and Employment Development (LEED) Working Papers, 2011/10, OECD Publishing. http://dx.doi.org/10.1787/5kg3mkv3tr21-en.

Froy, F. and S. Giguère (2010), "Putting in Place Jobs that Last: A Guide to Rebuilding Quality Employment at Local Level", OECD Local Economic and Employment Development (LEED) Working Papers, No. 2010/13, OECD Publishing. http://dx.doi.org/10.1787/5km7jf7qtk9p-en.

Government of Ireland (2014), "Action Plan for Jobs", Department of the Taoiseach, Dublin.

Government of Ireland (2012, 2013, 2014) "Pathways to Work: Government Policy Statement on Labour Market Activation", Department of the Taoiseach, Dublin.

Government of Ireland (2007), "National Action Plan for Social Inclusion 2007-2016", Stationery Office, Dublin.

Government of Ireland (1997), "Sharing in Progress – National Anti-Poverty Strategy", Stationery Office, Dublin.

Grangegorman Development Agency (undated) "Grangegorman Employment Charter: Guidelines for Contractors on the Implementation and Monitoring of the Grangegorman Employment Charter", www.ggda/employment-and-training.

Haase and Pratschke (2012), "The 2011 Pobal HP Deprivation Index for Small Areas (SA)". https://www.pobal.ie/Pages/New-Measures.aspx.

Hillier, B & Sahbaz, O. (2009), "An evidence based approach to crime and urban design", in Cooper, R and Evans, G and Boyko, C, (eds.) *Designing Sustainable Cities: Decision-making Tools and Resources for Design*, (163 - 186), Wiley Blackwell.

Hulse and Pinnegar (2015), "Housing markets and socio-spatial disadvantage: an Australian perspective," prepared for the Australian Housing and Urban Research Institute. http://www.ahuri.edu.au/publications/download/ahuri_myrp704_rp6.

Inter-Departmental Working Group 2015 *Report: Future Investment in Childcare in Ireland.* Dublin: Department of Children and Youth Affairs.

Jennings, P. (2013), "Melting the Iceberg of Fear: A Collective Response", Safer Blanchardstown, Dublin.

Lamech, S. (2014), "Evidence Strategy : The Danish Approach", *Presentation at LEED expert seminar on Tackling Disadvantage*, OECD Conference Centre, Paris, October 2014, http://www.oecd.org/cfe/leed/experts-tackling-disadvantage-paris.htm

McCulloch, L., Beasley, S., and Rourke, S. (2010), "An Overview of Community Safety in Blanchardstown RAPID Areas", Blanchardstown RAPID Community Safety Research, http://www.drugsandalcohol.ie/19657/1/Blanchardstown_local_community_safety.pdf.

Meath County Council (undated) "Meath County Development Plan 2013-2019, Volume 1", Written Statement, Meath County Council, Meath.

Mendell, M (2010) "Improving social inclusion at the local level through the social economy: Designing an enabling policy framework", *OECD Local Economic and Employment Development (LEED) Working Papers*, OECD Publishing, Paris, http://www.oecd.org/employment/leed/Improving-Social-Inclusion-Capacity.pdf.

Mendell, M., et al. (2009), "Improving Social Inclusion at the Local Level Through the Social Economy: Report for Poland", *OECD Local Economic and Employment Development (LEED) Working Papers*, No. 2009/01, OECD Publishing, Paris, http://dx.doi.org/10.1787/5kg0nvg0pnnt-en.

Morgenroth, E. (2012), 'ESRI Research Note: The Regional Dimension of the Unemployment Crisis', Quarterly Economic Quarterly,Winter: 61-73.

Munoz, S.A. Dr., Prof. J. Farmer, K. Stephen et al. (n.d.), "Achieving Social Enterprise Development in Rural Communities", O4O Policy Briefing No. 2., http://www.o4os.eu/userfiles/file/_General_Documents/Policy%20Briefing%202.pdf.

Neffke F., Henning M. (2013). Skill relatedness and firm diversification. Strategic Management Journal 34(3): 297-316.

Neffke, F., Henning, M. and Boschman, R. (2011) How do regions diversify over time? Industry relatedness and the development of new growth paths in regions. *Economic Geography*, Vol. 87, No. 3, pp. 237-265.

Noya, A.(ed.) (2009), *The Changing Boundaries of Social Enterprises*, Local Economic and Employment Development (LEED), OECD Publishing, Paris, http://dx.doi.org/10.1787/9789264055513-en.

Ó Broin, D. (2012). "Social enterprise or social entrepreneurship: economic solidarity or market hegemony"; in Doyle, G. and Lalor, T. (eds.) *Social Enterprise in Ireland: A People's Economy?*, pp. 19-28.

O'Donoghue, C., Geoghegan, C., Heanue, K. & Meredith, D. (2014) 'The Economic Structure of Towns in Ireland', *Journal of the Statistical and Social Inquiry Society of Ireland*, Vol. XLIII.

OECD LEED (forthcoming): OECD LEED HEInnovate Reviews: Universities, Entrepreneurship and Local Development; Country-Level Review Ireland Universities, Entrepreneurship and Local Development; Country-Level Review Ireland.

OECD (2016 forthcoming), "Report on Boosting Social Entrepreneurship and Social Entreprise Creation in Croatia".

OECD (2015a), OECD Economic Surveys: Ireland 2015, OECD Publishing, Paris, http://dx.doi.org/10.1787/eco_surveys-irl-2015-en.

OECD (2015b), *All on Board: Making Inclusive Growth Happen*, OECD Publishing, Paris, http://dx.doi.org/10.1787/9789264218512-en.

OECD (2015c), *Employment and Skills Strategies in Flanders, Belgium*, OECD Reviews on Local Job Creation, OECD Publishing, Paris. http://dx.doi.org/10.1787/9789264228740-en

OECD (2014a), *Employment and Skills Strategies in Ireland*, OECD Reviews on Local Job Creation. OECD Publishing, Paris, http://dx.doi.org/10.1787/9789264207912-en.

OECD (2014b), "Local Youth Employment Strategies: Ireland". Local Economic and Employment Development (LEED), Paris, http://www.oecd.org/cfe/leed/Youth-Local-Strategies-Ireland.pdf.

OECD (2014c), *Employment and Skills Strategies in Australia*, OECD Reviews on Local Job Creation, OECD Publishing, Paris. http://dx.doi.org/10.1787/9789264207899-en

OECD (2014d), *Job Creation and Local Economic Development*, OECD Publishing, Paris, http://dx.doi.org/10.1787/9789264215009-en.

OECD (2014e), *Innovation and modernising the rural economy*, OECD Publishing, Paris, http://dx.doi.org/10.1787/9789264205390-en.

OECD/EU (2013), *Policy Brief on Social Entrepreneurship: entrepreneurial activities in Europe*, EU /OECD, Publication Office of the European Union, Luxemburg, http://www.oecd.org/cfe/leed/Social%20entrepreneurship%20policy%20brief%20EN_FINAL.pdf.

OECD (2013a), *Demographic transition and an ageing society: Implications for local labour markets in Poland*, Local Economic and Employment Development (LEED), OECD Publishing, Paris, http://www.oecd.org/cfe/leed/Demographic_poland_report.pdf.

OECD (2013b), "Innovative Financing and Delivery Mechanisms for Getting the Unemployed into Work", OECD LEED Forum on Partnerships and Local Development Handbook #7, http://www.oecd.org/site/leedforumsite/publications/FPLD-handbook7.pdf.

OECD (2013c), *Local Strategies for Youth Employment*, OECD, Paris, www.oecd.org/employment/leed/local-strategies-youth-employment.htm.

OECD (2010a), *Breaking Out of Policy Silos: Doing More with Less*, Local Economic and Employment Development (LEED), OECD Publishing, Paris, http://dx.doi.org/10.1787/9789264094987-en.

OECD (2010b), "Social Entrepreneurship and Social Innovation", in OECD, *SMEs, Entrepreneurship and Innovation*, OECD Publishing, Paris, http://dx.doi.org/10.1787/9789264080355-50-en.

OECD (2010c), *OECD Territorial Reviews: Sweden 2010*, OECD Publishing, Paris, http://dx.doi.org/10.1787/9789264081888-en.

OECD (2006), *The New Rural Paradigm: Policies and Governance*, OECD Publishing, Paris. http://dx.doi.org/10.1787/9789264023918-en.

OECD (1999), Social Enterprises, OECD, Paris. http://dx.doi.org/10.1787/9789264182332-en.

OECD and German Ministry of Food Agriculture and Consumer Protection (2008), "Innovative Service Delivery – Meeting the Challenges of Rural Regions", OECD Rural Policy Conference, Cologne, 2008, http://www.oecd.org/gov/regional-policy/Innovative-Service-Delivery.pdf

Quigley, M., Gardner, C. & Dermody, A. (2013), "Working for Children: An Audit of Services and Needs Analysis of Children's Services in County Meath", Meath Children's Services Committee, Navan.

Robson, B.T., Lymperopoulou, K. and Rae, A. (2008) 'People on the move: exploring the functional roles of deprived neighbourhoods', Environment and Planning A, 40, 2693–1714.

Ryan, C. (2014), "Follow Up Survey of 2010 Enterprise Clients", Blanchardstown Area Partnership, Dublin.

Ryan, C. (2012), "Social and Economic Profile of Dublin 15", Blanchardstown Area Partnership, Dublin.

Sen, A. (1999), *Development as Freedom*, Oxford: University Press.

Skinner, G. (2012), "Department of Innovation, Business and Rural Development, Government of Newfoundland and Labrador", OECD Conference, October 2012, http://www.oecd.org/rural/krasnoyarsk/3%20Gillian%20Skinner_MR2_Skill%20Building_ENG.pdf.

Smyth, E., McCoy, S. & Kingston, G. (2015), "Learning from the Evaluation of DEIS", Economic and Social Research Institute, Dublin.

Social Entrepreneurship Network (n.d.), "Policy meets practice. Enabling the growth of social enterprises", Results of the Social Entrepreneurship Network – an ESF learning network 2013-14, Polish Ministry of Infrastructure and Development, http://socialeconomy.pl/sites/default/files/files/Social%20Entrepreneurship%20Network_final_Publication.pdf.

Spear, R. et al. (2010), "Improving Social Inclusion at the Local Level Through the Social Economy: Report for Slovenia", OECD Local Economic and Employment Development (LEED) Working Papers, 2010/16, OECD Publishing. http://dx.doi.org/10.1787/5kg0nvfx2g26-en.

Tochtermann L. and Clayton N. (2011), "Moving on up or moving on out? Overcoming the jobs-skills mismatch", Centre for Cities, http://www.centreforcities.org/wp-content/uploads/2014/09/11-07-05-Moving-on-up-moving-on-out-Overcoming-the-jobs-skills-mismatch.pdf.

Urry, J. (2007), Mobilities, Cambridge, Polity.

van Egeraat, C. & Gleeson, J. (2013), "Economic Baseline Study: Meath Local Authority June 2013", Meath County Council and AIRO.

Walsh, K. and Harvey, B, (2013), "Employment and Social Inclusion in Rural Areas: A Fresh Start", prepared for Pobal, Dublin, https://www.pobal.ie/Publications/Documents/Employment%20and%20Social%20Inclusion%20in%20Rural%20Areas%20-%20A%20Fresh%20Start.pdf.

Watson, D. & Maître, B. (2013), "Social Transfers and Poverty Alleviation in Ireland: An Analysis of the CSO Survey on Income and Living Conditions 2004-2011", Department of Social Protection and Economic and Social Research Institute, Dublin.

What Works Network (2014), https://www.gov.uk/what-works-network.

White House Council (2013), "Strong Cities, Strong Communities Initiative", *1st Annual Report*, April 2013, http://www.huduser.org/portal/publications/pdf/huddoc.pdf.

ORGANISATION FOR ECONOMIC CO-OPERATION AND DEVELOPMENT

The OECD is a unique forum where governments work together to address the economic, social and environmental challenges of globalisation. The OECD is also at the forefront of efforts to understand and to help governments respond to new developments and concerns, such as corporate governance, the information economy and the challenges of an ageing population. The Organisation provides a setting where governments can compare policy experiences, seek answers to common problems, identify good practice and work to co-ordinate domestic and international policies.

The OECD member countries are: Australia, Austria, Belgium, Canada, Chile, the Czech Republic, Denmark, Estonia, Finland, France, Germany, Greece, Hungary, Iceland, Ireland, Israel, Italy, Japan, Korea, Luxembourg, Mexico, the Netherlands, New Zealand, Norway, Poland, Portugal, the Slovak Republic, Slovenia, Spain, Sweden, Switzerland, Turkey, the United Kingdom and the United States. The European Union takes part in the work of the OECD.

OECD Publishing disseminates widely the results of the Organisation's statistics gathering and research on economic, social and environmental issues, as well as the conventions, guidelines and standards agreed by its members.

LOCAL ECONOMIC AND EMPLOYMENT DEVELOPMENT (LEED)

The OECD Programme on Local Economic and Employment Development (LEED) has advised governments and communities since 1982 on how to respond to economic change and tackle complex problems in a fast-changing world. Its mission is to contribute to the creation of more and better quality jobs through more effective policy implementation, innovative practices, stronger capacities and integrated strategies at the local level. LEED draws on a comparative analysis of experience from the five continents in fostering economic growth, employment and inclusion. For more information on the LEED Programme, please visit *www.oecd.org/cfe/leed*.

OECD PUBLISHING, 2, rue André-Pascal, 75775 PARIS CEDEX 16
(84 2016 03 1 P) ISBN 978-92-64-25266-0 – 2016

www.ingramcontent.com/pod-product-compliance
Ingram Content Group UK Ltd.
Pitfield, Milton Keynes, MK11 3LW, UK
UKHW051504290926
15471UKWH00008B/1405

9 789264 252660